AA Around the World:

Adventures in
Recovery

THE AA GRAPEVINE, INC.
NEW YORK, NEW YORK

OTHER BOOKS BY THE AA GRAPEVINE, INC.:

The Language of the Heart
Best of the Grapevine
Best of the Grapevine, Volume 2
Best of the Grapevine, Volume 3
The Home Group: Heartbeat of AA

IN SPANISH:

El Lenguaje del Corazón

Copyright© 2000 by The AA Grapevine, Inc.,
PO Box 1980, Grand Central Station,
New York, NY 10163-1980

Second Printing, 2005

Library of Congress Control Number: 00-090984

ISBN 0-933685-31-9
Printed in the United States of America

AA Around the World:

Adventures in Recovery

THE AA GRAPEVINE, INC.
NEW YORK, NEW YORK

The AA Preamble

Alcoholics Anonymous® is a fellowship
of men and women who share
their experience, strength and hope
with each other that they may solve
their common problem and help others
to recover from alcoholism.
The only requirement for membership
is a desire to stop drinking.
There are no dues or fees for
AA membership; we are self-supporting
through our own contributions.
AA is not allied with any sect,
denomination, politics, organization or
institution; does not wish to engage in
any controversy, neither endorses
nor opposes any causes.
Our primary purpose is to stay sober
and help other alcoholics
to achieve sobriety.

Contents

Preface

In the relatively short span of time since 1935, AA has crossed innumerable boundaries of language, culture, race, and geography, and reached alcoholics around the globe. This anthology of articles, reprinted from the AA Grapevine magazine, catalogs some of that incredible expansion and serves as a testament to the uncanny and universal ability of alcoholics to get and stay sober under extraordinary conditions.

Writing ten years after his first visit to European AA with his wife Lois in 1950, AA co-founder Bill W. had this to say: "As we journeyed from land to land, we had the same magnificent adventure in kinship over and over again. In Britain we met with the most wonderful love and understanding. In Ireland we were at one with the Irish. Everywhere, everywhere, it was the same. This was something much greater than people cordially meeting people. This was no merely interesting comparison of mutual experiences and aspirations. This was far more; this was the communication of heart to heart in wonder, in joy, and in everlasting gratitude. Lois and I then knew that AA could circle the globe — and it has."

As you read through the many experiences contained in this book, we can only hope that your adventure will be similar to the adventure described by Bill.

— The Editor

Part One

Making Meetings

THE EVER-BLOOMING ONE

Curaçao, Netherlands Antilles

This is the story of a group — how it started and how it grew and how it became the Ever-Blooming Group of Curaçao in the Netherlands Antilles. It is also the story of every group everywhere, and so it contains the ever old, ever new, and always magic ingredients of an AA real-life fairy tale.

It started in February 1956, when a returning traveler asked General Service Headquarters to send some literature to a fellow alcoholic he had met during a recent trip around the world. By early March we had a new and very enthusiastic Loner registered and a new pin added to the AA global map. Not long after, our fledgling wrote: "No matter how hard I try to help others in my community, no one will click — notwithstanding that I know and see the fellow killing himself with drink."

By July, after a brisk correspondence with Headquarters, Pedro was a fully occupied and active member. He had received the Big Book and *Twelve Steps and Twelve Traditions*, had become a subscriber to the Grapevine, and had on hand a selection of pamphlets, including those translated into Dutch and Spanish, since prospects existed who spoke both languages. In July, he wrote: "I am very sorry that I have to let you wait so long for a letter, but I had figured out that before writing you I must be very sure of our new group and also giving it a name; so yesterday we had our first official meeting and we are five, the Ever-Blooming Group. I hope that our group soon will be increasing in members for the whole island population is interested in our new way of living without alcohol."

The Ever-Blooming ones held their first open meeting sometime in November. Their founder describes it: "It was the first time in my life that I spoke sober in front of so many people, and you can imagine how terribly excited I was at the beginning, but once I started I have felt something very strange inside me, and so I kept on speaking for fifteen minutes! How AA can change a human being. Now we are in total eight members and hope that all of us some day will be top-flight AA members."

During the following months, we kept track of Pedro's progress through his correspondence. His unfailing good humor and gratitude expressed with graceful courtesy always charmed us; and so it was a special delight when we found the following letter dated April 14th of this year: "Dear Anita, I beg you to pardon me for not replying earlier. On the 24th I have been to Aruba to attend an AA meeting and there I also have been to the first Caribbean conference on mental health. It was a great success for our group, because now that the prominent figures of our community know our existence they are giving us their full cooperation and by that, our group in a few weeks has grown from eleven to thirty-four members. You can imagine how happy I am feeling. I have met an AA member from Beverly Hills, California named Jack W. — the first time I have spoken to an AA from the States! You can imagine my joy at this moment. I'm on vacation and will be in New York around May 14 with the tourist ship Santa Paula." And only a little over a year ago Pedro had despaired of ever "clicking" with any member of his community.

We met Pedro and his wife and teenage daughter at Headquarters soon after his arrival. It was a lovely occasion — one of those very special times when all of the grace and blessings this program can bestow shines in a concentrated glow from one happy family.

We told Pedro we would like to have his story when he returned from his vacation and had the time to write it. He was concerned about his ability to express himself in English, but he promised to do his best and with a refusal to take the easy way he sent us the following manuscript a few days before he sailed for home. He begged us to change "the things that are superfluous" and to correct his "horrible English." We have not changed one word.

PEDRO'S STORY

What a pleasant release I feel now when I proclaim that I am an alcoholic, because through this blessed fellowship Alcoholics Anonymous I have learned that alcoholism is an illness and how it can be arrested.

If, before I met AA, anyone had called me an alcoholic, I should have considered that person as my greatest enemy, for in my country the word alcoholic means an insult to a person. I think I was born an alcoholic, for at the age of fifteen I started drinking and I liked the stuff, so I kept on drinking for thirty years, almost every day till I found AA.

In my early years I had much fun out of drinking, but in my later years I became very shy and nervous, so I think now, that was the reason that I was spending so much money playing the big shot — to feel myself at home among other people and many times I have tried to stop drinking but I could not. Always after those heavy drinking bouts or after those difficulties I have been in through drinking, I promised my family and my employers that I'll never drink again, but those promises never endured even for twenty-four hours. I knew and I felt that my life was no good and that I was making many people, whom I love dearly, suffer through my drinking, but I also was thinking that life without alcohol was an impossibility. In my country Alcoholics Anonymous was unknown, or maybe it was known to other people but I never heard about it.

One day in September 1955 I was working on board a U.S. ship laying in our port. We — customs officers — used to have our meals with passengers in the dining hall, but that blessed morning I couldn't touch my breakfast, as always after those heavy drinking bouts. So I left the dining room and went out on the bridge to think over how to approach the ship's steward to get a drink out of him, and there I met AA in the person of Frank from Fremont, Ohio, a man who was a passenger on board that ship.

Between conversation he asked me why I didn't eat at the table and there I told him about my drinking and how much I wanted to stop, so he also told me his story about his drinking and how AA helped him. That was the first time I heard about help to stop drinking, because many times people have told me that I had to stop and I knew also that I must do something too, but nobody ever before told me about help, and now this man is talking about help.

This blessed man stayed on board the ship talking with me instead of going ashore shopping with his wife and other passengers. I know that I never can pay him back for what he has done for me that day, because although I didn't stop drinking then (for at first I didn't believe him), his words kept bouncing back in my mind every time after a drinking bout.

He kept writing me, sending AA pamphlets and books and he introduced me to the AA headquarters in New York, but it was almost six months later through studying the AA program I could make that decision to give myself over entirely to the care of my God, to take from me that drinking habit — and from the moment I made that decision I didn't feel that urge for a drink anymore.

After some time of sobriety, I felt I could not keep this happiness alone, so I started talking AA with my friends with whom I used to drink. I have been laughed at and many times they told me I was crazy, but through the encouragement I was receiving from my friends in the States, I kept trying to adjust my life the AA way, always trying to help someone I was thinking needed AA. By the Grace of God, one day two of my old friends clicked with me and we had our first meeting and so AA started in our country.

I made a promise, that since I was able to save the money I used to throw away during my drinking, I would make a trip to the U.S.A. whenever I got the opportunity, to meet the man who first mentioned AA to me and to see with my own eyes how AA works there and live for awhile among those AA friends who helped me so much to be what I am today.

God granted me that opportunity and I have lived for two months among my AA friends in different States of the U.S.A. and I had the most unforgettable wonderful experience of my life and I think that there is not another fellowship in this world with so much under-standing and kindness. God bless AA.

Pedro
(September 1957)

'IN A BAMBOO HOUSE ON STILTS'

Maryknoll, New York

All my adult life, owing to my line of work, I've had to travel to some pretty isolated spots in the world. About nineteen years ago, my Higher Power caught up with me, and unexpectedly I found myself in the rooms of Alcoholics Anonymous. When I'd reached the ripe old age of six months in the program, I was asked to go on assignment to the "Green Hell," the Amazon jungles of Bolivia. Unsure of myself, and feeling sort of wobbly about my fledgling sobriety, I asked my sponsor, Jim, for advice. "What should I do?" He assured me that if I was doing the will of my Higher Power and if, through prayer and meditation, I were to stay in contact with God and with my sponsor, God wouldn't let me get into a situation where I couldn't remain sober. He would always be there to lend me a hand and to give me strength when I felt I was growing weak. Jim pointed out that the name of the game was "trust." "Are you ready to turn your will and your life over to the Higher Power?" he asked. His final words of advice were, "Remember, Dan, easy does it." But as I made arrangements to head for South America, I thought, "What if Jim is wrong?"

To my surprise and delight, Jim had told me the truth! Three months later, I returned from the jungle sunburned and mosquito-bitten but with my sobriety still intact, if not strengthened.

And now, nearly two decades of sobriety later, I am still "on the road." Not too many months ago, I spent nine weeks on assignment in Southeast Asia, and was badly in need of an AA meeting. I'd attended a large meeting in a church hall in hot and sultry Bangkok, Thailand, and had been to another smaller one on a sunny front porch in Phnom Penh, Cambodia. But two meetings in two months was not enough. Since leaving Cambodia, I'd traipsed around the steamy wilds of Borneo in Malaysia. Everywhere I went, I looked in vain for an AA meeting. I did a lot of praying and meditating, but I could find no meeting. I really needed to talk to someone who would understand an alcoholic who was turning a bit raggedy around the travel-worn edges.

That was on my mind as the dugout canoe in which I was riding made its way across the crocodile-infested waters to the town of Agats in Irian Jaya. If you're not-quite sure where that is, take out your atlas and find a map of the South Pacific. There you will locate the island of New Guinea just north of Australia. Then look at the western half of the island — the part which belongs to Indonesia. That side is the province of Irian Jaya; on the southwest coast, on the Arafura Sea, where the Asmat people live, is the little settlement of Agats.

In this remote corner of the globe, it seemed an even remoter possibility that I would find an AA meeting. The canoe pulled up to shore, and I waded across the squishy mudflats, gratefully heading for dry land. It had been arranged that I would stay with some Catholic missionaries there in the village. Meeting me graciously at the shore, they demonstrated their hospitality by offering me a cold beer. I thanked them for their offer but opted for lemonade instead.

Several hours later, I found myself seated in the missionaries' dining room, having supper with them. The conversation ebbed and flowed around me, and I gradually grew drowsy in the equatorial heat. But all of a sudden, one of my table mates, James, said, "As we say, easy does it. . . ." A shock ran through me. After the meal ended, the missionaries headed off to their various chores and I followed James outside to ask, "You wouldn't be a friend of Bill's would you?" Grinning, he nodded.

That evening, in a bamboo house on stilts above the tidal waters of the Arafura Sea, James and I had a meeting, accompanied by the rhythmic drumming of the Asmat people who were celebrating a local feast. The collective wisdom of Bill and Bob, and the voices of so many uncounted members over the past sixty years wrapped around us in the tropical night. It was a lesson in trust.

Daniel J.
(January 1996)

CAMINO A LA SOBRIEDAD

Islas de la Bahia, Honduras

On the third pull of the starter cord, the outboard motor purrs reassuringly. The moon is just coming up over the horizon as I back the dinghy away from the dock. The Southeast trade winds are blowing afresh. The harbor is choppy — whitecaps are everywhere. I try to stay in the lee. If the Higher Power sees to it that the spark plugs won't foul just now, it looks as if I'll actually make the meeting on time.

After crossing the harbor, then up a canal, then across an open stretch of water, I finally dock up. Then comes the trek on foot by flashlight down the muddy path. At this time, our group's name is recalled, if a bit ruefully, as I slosh through a puddle — "Camino a la Sobriedad" (Pathway to Sobriety).

There are four of us when everybody shows up. We're a new group, less than a year old. We're kind of a nefarious bunch of wanderers who have found a safe haven from the turbulent sea of alcoholism. Me, I've lived aboard boats for about eleven years. Then there's Fernando, the Nicaraguan refugee, and José and Don Antonio, two *costeños*, men from the mainland (the "coast") who have moved here to the Bay Islands in search of a better life. By day, José can be seen in the bush hacking vines, which he bends into a thick sort of wicker. He makes furniture sets. By night, he becomes a man of the mountains — with kerosene lantern and pick axe, he roams the hills in search of buried treasure.

Like a light at the end of a tunnel, the warm glow of our flickering kerosene lamp greets me as I enter our little *casita*. "Little" is both an affectionate term and a descriptive one. We could seat about six or eight if everybody is really friendly. Everything is green inside — electric green. The benches, the table, the lectern. We say our *buenos noches* and wait, expectantly. Will somebody new come tonight?

After a polite grace period filled with the day's happenings, we begin our meeting. Two sharp raps on the bell, our prize acquisition. Nobody knows exactly how it got here, but it adds a certain air of respectability, of authority. It's the kind of bell you ring at hotel counters when you want to be waited on. We rise to our feet, heads bowed. The ceiling is very low.

Our moment of silence is again punctuated by the bell, the signal to be seated. We then read the Preamble, followed by the Twelve Steps and Twelve Traditions. Clomp, clomp, clomp. We hear somebody on the steps outside. The gait doesn't sound too steady, nor too regular. Could it be a drunk? A bewhiskered face peers in. The goat has chewed through his rope again. No — out! You can't come in here! You're not an alcoholic. Oh, that goat! What fine company he has been to me on the nights when the "regulars" failed to show up.

We share our room with a family of rats, plus assorted tarantulas and scorpions. About once a meeting somebody suddenly gets up and sort of karate-kicks the wall. At times it just ain't easy to be tolerant of all God's critters.

We take turns at *la tribuna* (the podium). It was hard, at first, never having spoken at a group before, for me to express my innermost feelings in a language that is not my primary one. It was difficult, too, as a woman alcoholic in a traditional Latin culture. But they smiled me into sobriety, loved me back when I slipped and slid, and cared like no one else could. We'd all been paddling the same dugout canoe toward death, when two gringos long ago in that faraway "United of States" started this sober channel for us.

There's a humility here unknown to me in the States, where if there wasn't plenty of everything, there was usually at least enough of the basics. Words like gratitude take on stronger meaning. My bronze, barefoot peasant friends have shown me what quality sobriety is all about.

When the Seventh Tradition is announced, the broken shell of an electrician's "trouble light" is passed. Whew! We've collected enough, at last, to pay the rent, and we have a surplus of 80 centavos (40¢). Ah, our prudent reserve.

We work; we struggle; we will survive. We know each other's stories. We hope for new blood. We hope for our brothers and sisters, our neighbors and friends in need of this lifesaving program.

We pause for coffee. A cacophony of sounds surrounds us: next door there is feverish hymn-singing and clapping of hands; across the street are the painful wails and screaming of a wake; babies are crying; and in the apartment on the other side of the wall, Bob Marley reminds us that we are all one world, one people.

We, too, are united, as we close our meeting with the Serenity Prayer, standing, heads bowed. It's a low ceiling.

B. C.
(January 1988)

PILGRIMS TO THE CASTLE

Spokane, Washington

My wife and I, both members of AA, along with our two teenage children, had spent the entire fall in Romania, in eastern Europe along the Soviet border, far from our home-based source of spiritual strength in Washington State, U.S.A. We had brought the Big Book and other AA literature with us, and the two of us had founded Grupa Una in Romania. It usually met on Sunday morning in our bedroom, where we played tapes of meetings friends had sent from home, or Bill W.'s tape on the Legacies. Though half a world away from our AA family, we felt their strength and love on these tapes and through a constant stream of supportive letters and occasional phone calls.

The wonderful people in our host country found us difficult to understand at times. Raised to believe that alcohol was a necessary part of each day's midday supper and late-evening dinner, they invited us to their homes and expected us to enjoy both food and drink. We often ended up speaking at length about AA (of which they knew nothing), trying to explain why we didn't want anything to drink: "No thank you," not even a "thimbleful" of *tuica*, the national drink, a kind of plum brandy. Finally convinced that we could indeed have a wonderful time without drinking, our hosts would relax and let us be as we happily sipped *apa minerala*, an excellent nonalcoholic soda water.

We decided to spend Christmas in Vienna, en route to London, where my wife and children were scheduled to take off for home. The children needed to be back in school, and my wife's place was with them. So on a dark, cold morning in Romania, we caught the famous Orient Express. We rocked westward through the frozen plains of eastern Hungary to Budapest and then farther to the west on this intriguing train which carried travelers from both East and West, a polyglot troupe speaking languages and dialects from the Orient and Europe.

At last, we came to Vienna in the West, to bright lights and pastries and shops stuffed with goods of every imaginable sort — and to the strong possibility of an AA meeting! We pored over the International AA Directory in our hotel, located close to Karntner Strasse, Vienna's magnificent shopping district, and St. Stephen's, the fabled Gothic cathedral. We found a telephone number and made the call. To our delight, we were soon talking in English to an AA member whose buoyant, cheerful voice and sense of AA humor immediately brought tears to our eyes — tears of identification and recognition. "Yes, of course," he said, "there's a wonderful meeting tonight at the old castle off Thalia Strasse. Just take the trolley toward the Danube on Neubaugartel, get off at Lerchenfelder, and then take the Thalia Strasse trolley to the woods. From there, you'll have to walk." He gave us the address.

That evening, with four or five inches of snow on the ground and more falling, we set out bravely to find the castle. The journey to Lerchenfelder along the Neubaugartel was not difficult, but when we got off the trolley and realized we must now find the woods somewhere along Thalia Strasse, we were at a loss. Which direction along Thalia Strasse? And how far? We stood there in the snowfall — Christmas was just a few days ahead — and wondered what to do. Nearby, at the corner, perhaps a hundred Austrians stood waiting for various trams or trolleys. We were all cold, the snow falling in big sticky flakes.

The Austrians stood hunched over, self-absorbed, waiting for the right vehicle to come along. "Perhaps someone there can help us," I said to my wife, and we walked over to the crowd. For some reason, I noticed a woman holding a small child asleep in her arms. Was there something different about her? Did she look up as I approached? I walked up to her and said, "Do you speak English?"

"Yes," she said, and smiled.

"We're trying to find a wooded area off Thalia Strasse somewhere," I said. "Could you possibly help us?"

She looked at me quizzically, and then a light seemed to glow in her eyes, and her face softened. "Tell me," she said gently, "are you trying to find an old castle by eight-thirty tonight?"

I gasped, "Yes," and my wife and I stood there long in the silent snow, both realizing that once again in our AA lives, we had been struck by the strange lightning that can sometimes make the hair rise on the back of your neck, the lightning that generates a sudden, vital insight, or seems to tear into ribbons the expected natural laws of coincidence — the special AA lightning that we AAs learn to accept, to look for, even to expect. We needed very much to find that meeting in the Austrian castle, and Margaret (for that's what I shall call her) — was there for us, standing in the snow with her child asleep in her arms. We found out later she was the only person in that one hundred or so waiting who was also going to the AA meeting.

Margaret guided us to the right trolley, and we soon found ourselves in the dark outskirts of Vienna. We got off the trolley and began walking through the woods, up a gentle hill along a narrow, curving roadway. Above us and ahead, we could see the rampart and parapet of the castle, and soon we were in the main hall, shaking snow from our clothing, happy to be warm and snug within the thick walls. My wife and I looked at each other. We knew we would never have found the castle without Margaret's help.

And the meeting was joyful, in an ancient, oak-beamed room, high in a corner of the castle. There were twelve of us, and the secretary made the mistake of asking me to chair. I just couldn't stop talking, and laughing, and crying. My wife and I had subconsciously saved up uncounted anecdotes of our adventures throughout the fall in

Romania, many of them having to do with our AA perceptions, and now they poured out in an intense emotional release. We were blessed with a most tolerant group of AAs that evening; they let us talk and talk until finally we ran down, so relieved and content that we had finally been able to share our experiences with other AA members.

The topic for the meeting was gratitude — a topic perfect for our needs and particularly appropriate that night, with Christmas just ahead. The group was composed primarily of Austrians, but also some other Europeans now living and working in Austria, two people from England, and one from Africa. All spoke in English, now certainly the accepted second language of choice in most European countries. The Europeans in particular were interested in hearing about American AA — what the meetings were like, what AA members were like there — and we in turn were fascinated by European attitudes and perceptions.

What we all found out, before the meeting was half over, was that there was absolutely no difference among Europe or Africa or America in the way alcohol — beer or Scotch or schnapps or tuica — could insidiously work its way into the center of our beings and take full control. The stories we heard in the old Viennese castle were substantially the same stories of blackouts, family breakups, loss of financial and physical health, personal disasters, and despair that we would hear at meetings in America. We sat together sharing our experience strength, and hope — and together we felt the special presence that can be felt only in an AA meeting, that presence of joy and hope and faith and promise. We represented different countries, different continents, different cultures that night — but we were one in the spirit of AA, one in the knowledge that for us, the nightmare of alcoholism was over, one in the certainty that we could find purpose and meaning in our lives, just one day at a time, by wholeheartedly following AA's Steps and Traditions.

With much laughter and gaiety, we left for the hotel after the meeting, this time with six AAs who made sure we found the right trolley! My wife and I sat holding hands, looking out at the continuing snowfall. We were completely at peace, the tension of the months in eastern Europe drained out of us.

When we returned to the hotel, the children could see the peace in our faces. "Found a great meeting, didn't you!" one of them said. "You'll never believe it!" I replied. "You'll never believe it!"

F. P.
(December 1985)

A NOT-SO-SECRET SOCIETY

Dubai, United Arab Emirates

I would like to describe my experiences of starting AA meetings in an Islamic country. After seven years of recovery in London where there are hundreds of meetings every week, I and my wife (whom I met in AA and who has eleven years' sobriety) moved to Dubai in the Persian Gulf. We discovered that AA wasn't listed in the telephone directory — or anywhere else.

Eventually we found a handful of fellow AAs and four meetings a week. Two meetings were in a private clinic and two were held in the psychiatric ward of the state hospital. There had been a fifth meeting in one of the country's two Christian churches, but for no apparent reason the priest had begun to make it difficult for proper meetings to be held. The hospital would only permit meetings to take place if a psychologist, who was frequently disruptive, attended meetings. If an in-patient actually attended these open meetings, an armed guard also had to be present.

Not surprisingly, morale was very low. Without being specific about how official Islamic disapproval inhibited AA, I will say that many members who'd been here for a number of years believed that to survive, AA had to be a secret society. Anonymity, they asserted, had become a question of basic survival. But such extreme anonymity had also sounded the death knell for our Fifth Tradition and Twelfth Step.

I voiced my concern about this to another member, and he and I set about finding some new meeting venues. It was a humiliating experience. No one would cooperate. Even the other church would have nothing to do with Alcoholics Anonymous. An additional problem was that, unlike in the West where there is a sense of neighborhood manifested in community centers and halls attached to places of worship, here there were only massive resort-style hotel complexes.

I was at a complete loss, and so I had to turn it over. A week went by and the phone rang. It was Mike, a serviceman from one of the many U.S. Navy ships that put in here. After days of trying, he had eventually found one of our well-hidden meetings where I had given him my number. He now had a Twelfth Step prospect, a barman in a hotel downtown. Together, we met the barman, but he wasn't interested.

Back at my apartment I shared our problem with meeting venues with Mike. I told him that I intuitively felt that as all social and most commercial activity centers around the hotels, they were the logical place to hold meetings. However, I had never heard of an AA meeting being held in a hotel before and after the frosty reception we'd received at the other more obvious venues, I wasn't keen to lead with my chin again.

Just a year sober, Mike immediately asked me where it was that our Higher Power had chosen to directly intervene in the lives of our co-founders to create Alcoholics Anonymous? In a hotel, of course! He rang the top people in all the big hotels asking them if they were willing to help visiting U.S. servicemen. They were all happy to meet him. So we went in to see six of them; we introduced Alcoholics Anonymous and told them of our need. Four were delighted to help and we took two of them up on their kind offer.

We started two new meetings immediately and they were an instant success. Next we needed to advertise them. We went to see the USO, the American forces organization, which offered to set up a twenty-four-hour telephone information line for us. USO would overcome any official objections to AA that might exist by applying for the line in their name. We agreed to pay them a year in advance for the line rental.

With the line set up, we went around to the English-language newspapers and magazines and requested a daily or monthly listing. We explained who we were and why we needed it. Three out of four agreed with no discussion.

Already our meetings have grown in size and spirit. Newcomers can find us, and visiting business people and U.S. service people have swelled our meetings still further. We now have a meeting every day of the week, enabling new people to do ninety meetings in ninety days if they wish.

And above all I haven't found it necessary to take that first drink.

Hamish
(January 1996)

'IRONIES OF GRACE'

Zagreb, Croatia

When I was a young woman, I went to Rome to study music. By a quirky set of circumstances, I ended up living in an apartment in the manse of the American Episcopal Church on Via Napoli and Via Nazionale, a dwelling generally reserved for visiting bishops. It was a wonderful spot for me, not only because of its central location, but also because there was a beautiful old library upstairs that held a nine-foot Steinway grand, and I had the privilege of practicing there on a daily basis. My roommate was studying flute and we had a great time studying our music and hanging out with other young American artists and students, with actors from the Living Theater, and with Italians we got to know. This was during a period when my drinking was working very well for me, keeping terrifying feelings under a lid, and allowing me to bubble up as an artistic and social being.

On certain days, as we left our building to go out into the city, we noticed nondescript people coming in and heading for the basement. I thought nothing of it when the church secretary told me they were headed for a meeting of Alcoholics Anonymous.

All this made a fleeting impression on me. I completely forgot it for years — something like twenty-five years. Then I got sober. In spite of having professional reasons for going to Italy on a regular basis, I'd put it off until my sobriety had set in enough for me to feel comfortable returning to the site of so much of my drinking. Other people visit Rome and think about history, art, and politics. But when I returned to Rome sober, my itinerary was awash in memories of drinking: in this trattoria, in this piazza, in this café. I was thrilled to learn there were AA meetings in Rome, and I hopped in a taxi in order to get to one on time.

The taxi took me straight to my former address, the very building where I had done so much of my youthful drinking. Just as so many had done before me, I headed for the basement room. Someone asked me to chair the meeting and to tell my story. Part of it that day was about my former connection to the palazzo we were in and the irony of returning there as a member of AA. The others in the room laughed but hardly seemed surprised. I have learned that things like this happen all the time to those of us lucky enough to have found recovery. I call them ironies of grace.

Today I am experiencing yet another irony of grace. In my drinking days, during one of the periods when I was living in Italy, I once took a vacation trip up the Dalmatian coast of the former Yugoslavia. This is one of the most beautiful places on earth, and I remember parts of the trip vividly. One of my clear memories is of staying the night in a campground where my boyfriend and I met a Yugoslav family. They were incredibly friendly and hospitable, and we spent the day water-skiing on their boat. We did so much of that, I remember, that the next day our arms felt as if they were about to fall off, and we could barely steer our car. This sensation may also have had something to do with what we had drunk. The father of the family had ample quantities of home-made *slivovitz*, a fiery white liquid that really did the trick. I drank myself silly and woke up the next morning with a head that felt like it had been cloven in two. I don't remember what I did that night, but I remember how drunk I was. The next day's pain wasn't just from the water-skiing.

Now that I've been sober (to my amazement, and by grace) almost nine years, my life has undergone the many changes the Steps provide and the promises of sobriety are being fulfilled. My work, among other things, has taken new directions — well, relatively new. I'm back in the former Yugoslavia, in the nation-state of Croatia, to which I have returned for professional reasons related to humanitarian and scholarly work that have nothing to do with music.

My first trip back was in 1993, while the war was still raging. I came to Zagreb, the capital of Croatia, which was calm, and to which I would return three more times before the war ended. As I have learned to do when I travel, I looked in the phone book as soon as I could for anything that resembles Alcoholics Anonymous. I'm not very good in Croatian, but I did find a couple of numbers to call. I got a call back from a psychiatrist who spoke English and who ran one of the large recovery programs here. These programs are not AA-related and don't make use of the Twelve Steps and Twelve Traditions or any of our other tools. I must admit that I don't know how effective they are. They may work well for some people; I surely hope so.

My own experience, however, was to attend a meeting of a bunch of pretty wet-looking fellow alcoholics in a small room in one of Zagreb's suburbs. As an invited guest of the psychiatrist, I was asked to tell my story, so the folks at that meeting heard about the determining role of AA in my own recovery. I was surprised to learn that the psychiatrist who was leading the meeting was not himself an alcoholic. I also observed that the people who wanted to find sobriety looked at him for all their guidance rather than to each other, as we do. This psychiatrist, who I believe means well, explained to me that, since AA was "a religious program," there were countries "like Croatia and Latin America" where it "couldn't possibly work."

Well, it's attraction rather than promotion. Besides, who am I to know what other people need? All I can say for sure is what works for me. I left a Big Book with them and returned to my hotel, glad that I didn't have to drink.

The next day, while attempting to cross a busy street in the center of town, I saw that traffic had gotten jammed up at the intersection. Most of the drivers were taking this brief inconvenience with aplomb, but one man who just couldn't bear it was leaning on his horn, having what we might call a rage attack. I glanced over and saw that the furious noisemaker was none other than the psychiatrist upon whose sobriety and even serenity so many alcoholics seemed to depend. Now, I don't for one minute think that sober alcoholics never become angry. I am aware enough of my own experiences not to be that naive. But I must say that, at that moment, I was grateful beyond words that my own sobriety didn't depend on the angry psychiatrist, or on anyone else, for that matter. AA had given me a way to let God hold me up, traffic jam or no traffic jam. With the help of the Steps, I can turn my anger over. I can relax into God's strong support simply by recognizing it's there.

Four years have passed since then. The war has ended, Croatia is independent, and I have returned here to do the work I mentioned previously. I arrived at the beginning of February, and, although I'd planned to stay here for a year, I'd been pretty cavalier about seeing to my AA needs. I had come, for example, with no phone numbers and no International Directory. My sponsor was in California, and the closest meetings I knew about were in Venice, an eight-hour train trip away. I went dry for two and a half months. Then I decided to confide in someone I'd met at the U.S. Embassy, a person whom I thought I could trust with my story in general terms. We met in a café, I told him my story, and I asked him if he would be willing to place an ad anonymously in the embassy newsletter. He said that he had many friends who had been helped by AA; he would be glad to do so.

Next, on a trip back to the United States, I went to meetings during a stopover in Zurich. Here were sober alcoholics who attended regular meetings! The friendship they extended to me, which continues long distance over the phone and by E-mail, and whenever I can stop in Zurich, brought me back with a surge of warmth, and I recognized that I couldn't go on much longer in Zagreb without meetings. In New York, I visited the General Service Office and had some wonderful talks with the people who work there. They gave me a pamphlet about getting a meeting started. I found the suggested wording for an ad particularly helpful. I attended an AA meeting at GSO and other meetings all around Manhattan. I went to California, met with my sponsor, and attended meetings there. When I returned to Croatia, I knew what to do.

My embassy friend placed an ad in the newsletter that said, "Think you might have a problem with drinking? Perhaps Alcoholics Anonymous can help. Call [my phone number]." The next day I got a call from a young woman who had arrived in Zagreb two weeks earlier to work at the embassy. She had several years' sobriety and had been very keen to find a meeting and very worried that there might not be one. We had our first meeting together in the lobby of the Sheraton Hotel. Then she found another AA person, someone who had been living here for several years and who had grown hesitant to start a meeting out of a sense that to do so might put him at risk with official power structures. He came to our second meeting, where he expressed his relief and joy at being at a meeting again after several years.

A fourth alcoholic in recovery has turned up, and, since wonders never seem to cease, we now have a rent-free meeting place in the center of town, thanks once again to some inquiries made by our sympathetic friend at the embassy. It looks as if we've been given a wonderful opportunity to work the Twelfth Step, with a clear demonstration that the reason for doing so is always to improve the quality of our own sobriety first. None of us came to Zagreb with the intention of being AA missionaries; that would go against the principles of the program, and we are here for professional reasons. But now we are thinking of new ways to make our meeting times known to the English-speaking community here as well as of ways to make the program available to alcoholics who want to stop drinking and don't speak English. This Twelfth Step work, which none of us asked to do, has already been a terrific blessing to me.

I'd been under the assumption that no meetings had existed here before. Well, the other day I got a letter from a cloistered monk, an American, who lives in Slovenia and had found my address in the *Loners-Internationalists Meeting* publication. It turns out that he'd lived here in Zagreb several years before and had started up a meeting back then. When he left Croatia, however, the only other sober alcoholic he knew in the country was a German-speaking Croat who lives in a town just outside Zagreb. This Croat doesn't have a phone, but we're going to try to contact him, too.

Here's the point: our efforts won't be so historic after all, as we aren't the first sober alcoholics to hold AA meetings in this country. But being here now, when there are apparently no meetings other than the ones we hold, is an unexpected gift of sobriety. I came here worried about how I would maintain my spiritual life and keep up my sobriety. As it turns out, the Twelfth Step is suddenly my mainstay. It has brought me to a temporary sponsor here, to meetings that are getting ever more regular, to several other alcoholics who are working the AA program, and to a feeling of spiritual cushioning I surely needed and can get only through AA.

I want to sign off by sending my love and best wishes to all the members of my home group, The Happy Hour in Syracuse, New York, to all my old friends in California, in Palo Alto and Berkeley AA, where I got and stay sober, to my new friends in Zurich AA, and to all the members of the Fellowship who attend meetings who have helped me maintain my sobriety all over the world. I woke up today part of the miracle, and I have you and my God to thank for that.

Beverly A.
(December 1997)

New Beginnings in an Ancient Land

Tel Aviv, Israel

 started drinking seriously during Israel's war of liberation in the late nineteen-forties. My unit was stationed next to one of the most popular bars in the city. The city was under siege, food was scarce, but the British had left the city well provided with alcohol. Here I was with time on my hands, little to eat, and lots of booze. I drank in a big way. It didn't take long for me to find myself in a situation where I was unable to function without a drink.

After the war, I began doing very well as a radio broadcaster, even becoming quite a success. In fact, alcohol gave me the extra boost I needed to do my job. I was unable to go on the air without taking a little something to help me. At first it was in moderate quantities, but soon it was measured in bottles instead of single drinks. Then the idea of a glass as an intermediary between lips and bottle just vanished.

At this stage I still tried to keep up appearances. I used to fortify myself before going to places where too much drinking was not acceptable; at the event, usually part of my job, I drank little. However, I didn't always manage to stick to my good intentions. It wasn't too long before my alcohol arithmetic became hazy.

During this semi-hazy period I got attached to a woman who objected to my drinking. Her way of showing her dissatisfaction was by leaving me in a big and public way. This was humiliating and painful. Financially I was still solvent, but I was spending much more than I earned. I borrowed from family and friends. I begged for advance payment on my salary. I did every dirty trick to get money to support my drinking. Eventually my friends, colleagues, and family got weary of me.

However, I still managed to do a fairly good job and got a wonderful woman to marry me and have a daughter. In fact I did so well that I was sent to England. London was a drunkard's heaven. I had a small pocket flask, and I did systematic pub crawling. The bottle functioned as an energy resource to get me from one pub to the other in the cold English weather I wasn't accustomed to. That was an excellent excuse to drink as much as I wanted — to keep me warm. Many times I was unable to find my way home and I slept the night off in some sleazy hotel, in an unfamiliar neighborhood, from which it took me days to return to home and job. When the money ran out, I frequently found myself outside in the freezing cold.

When I returned to my homeland, I was already an accomplished drunk, a liar, a genius at sponging money, ready to do everything to buy the next drink, including bouncing and forging checks. When life became intolerable, I tried a geographic solution again. I still had my reputation, so I maneuvered for a job in Scandinavia, where I found even better reasons for drinking: it was even colder than England, a harsh and unwelcoming climate, a winter with long dark days. Then I was off to study in New York, exchanging aquavit for bourbon. I was having all sorts of health problems, some real, some imaginary, and some probably the result of heavy drinking. The doctor had no idea what to do with me.

How I managed to study and even graduate remains a mystery to me. After I graduated, I returned home via Lisbon. I was drinking heavily on the plane, mixing the alcohol with a good number of sleeping pills. Instead of getting home, I woke up in a Portuguese hospital, where nobody spoke any English. I found out later what had happened. At some stage I had asked the stewardess for another drink. I was very drunk and she refused and called the captain. At that time I weighed no more than 120 pounds, but I became violent. It took four strong men to overpower me and tie me down. They left me in a hospital during the stopover.

When I returned home, the bad times started with a vengeance. My drinking became totally uncontrollable. I lost family, money, job, home — I lost it all. I realized that I had a problem but thought there was nothing I could do about it. I became a regular patient in mental hospitals. I was fairly cooperative as long as I was hospitalized, but once I was discharged, I promptly began drinking again. I spent time in reasonably nice hospitals (I had nowhere to turn anyway) which provided food, shelter, and human company. I didn't have to worry about anything. It made drinking a bit complicated, but I managed. I was very good at faking it — most of the time. In those days, the doctors and nurses knew very little about alcoholism and were easily fooled. One psychologist told me that I was an alcoholic. And she knew from her studies and visits to North America that there was one thing that might help, and that was AA, but it didn't exist in Israel at that time.

I did not appreciate this simple diagnosis. I thought it was much more elegant to be diagnosed as suffering from "personality disorders" than just being a drunk. One day I booked myself into a cheap hotel with a few bottles and no food. I don't know how long I stayed there, probably about two weeks. I woke up in a hospital room with double pneumonia, losing thirty-five pounds. I understood that I was committing suicide in a slow and shameful way — so why not do it cleanly, in one swift act? I tried and failed even that. Then I got a call from my psychologist. She told me that she had read in a newspaper that some people had founded AA in Israel. She gave me a telephone number, and since I was desperate, I called immediately. I was told that these people were sitting at somebody's flat, chatting over a cup of coffee, and I was welcome to come along. Something made me go right then.

There were three of them: a local English-speaking woman and two Canadian army officers attached to the United Nations. They gave me the Big Book and some pamphlets. What they were saying made no sense to me, in fact it seemed very silly, but one thing did come through: the men were senior army officers, they were smartly dressed, clean-shaven, and neat. They didn't look like drunks, yet once we started talking they convinced me that they had been exactly where I was. They understood what I was talking about. They were once lost drunks like me and somehow they had stopped drinking. That was the message I took away from that gathering — not the literature, not the pamphlets, but the belief that here were drunks like me who had stopped. If they could make it, why not me too? I wanted what they had, whatever it was.

I haven't had a drink from that evening on. I don't know why, I don't know how. One of the two Canadians, Bob, became my sponsor and I owe him my life. I decided the following: I will commit suicide on the fifteenth of the month if things don't work out. I just didn't specify which month! In the meantime I attended meetings. AA became my family, my home, my friends, my religion.

In the first few months, I didn't say much, but I listened. I listened to my sponsor, to some guests from abroad who were old-timers, and to newcomers. I learned mostly from the newcomers, with whom I could easily identify. It wasn't easy. I was in my late forties. I had to reconstruct a life out of the ruins. It took time and it was extremely difficult and complicated. I advanced three steps and retreated two. It is a road that nobody can travel alone. Finally I built up a new family and made up with what was left of my old one. I started a new career and did well.

Whenever I start climbing the walls for some reason — usually because I'm unable to have things my way, like the behavior of my boss, my son's attitude, or even my country's politics — I have an instant cure. I close my eyes and visualize one of the many moments of past horror and humiliation: waking up in the street, begging a stranger for money, talking my way into buying a bottle on credit, or (worst of all) trying to convince a doctor to hospitalize me because I had nowhere to go. This and the Serenity Prayer always work instant magic.

When AA was first established in Israel, it was very intimate. We met in private homes. Meetings were held in English, and were therefore of limited value to those who were not bilingual. Eventually this changed. There was some internal bickering over the language issue. It was solved by a growing number of groups meeting both in Hebrew and in English.

The year 1995 was the climax of my AA life. I attended the International Convention in San Diego, together with some 80,000 other drunks, who looked happy and orderly and had a special aura about them. The friend in whose flat where I'd attended my first unofficial AA meeting twenty-three years before (and who has since left for greener pastures) proudly carried the flag of my country among the hundred flags from all over the globe. I went round in the convention, meeting people, talking to friends I'd just met, with one thought that would not let go: here I am with so many people from different countries, races, religions, professions, genders, and backgrounds, but they all — young and old, newcomers and old-timers — have been where I have been. And I had once thought I was all alone and nobody could share or understand what I'd experienced.

Moshe B.
(March 1999)

'There's a Seat for Me in Cuba'

New York, New York

I'm a lighting technician for a television news program. In January 1998, we were assigned to go to Cuba to cover Pope John Paul II's visit. At the time, I didn't know if AA meetings existed on this embargoed island, but I knew that finding AA in Cuba was going to be my first order of business.

Fortunately, I found several AA meetings listed in the International Directory as well as a telephone number for the AA intergroup in Havana. Immediately, my anxieties were alleviated — there would be somewhere in Cuba for me to go to get relief from my alcoholism. "This trip," I thought, "will be no problem. There is a seat waiting for me there."

The prospects of the trip were exciting and at the same time daunting, primarily because the very isolated nature of this country posed some technical and logistical considerations that were sure to present tremendous demands to our crew — and on my sobriety. From my four years of continuous sober experience, I was certain that the challenges of this trip would afford plenty of "opportunities for growth."

Upon arrival in Havana, we were faced with the realization that many of the problems we anticipated had, indeed, materialized. These worst-case scenarios were further complicated by the fact that most of our lighting crew had to be left behind in Mexico because their visas hadn't been approved in time; this left only myself and one other lighting technician to do the work of an entire lighting crew. Originally, our show had hired five local Cubans for the sole purpose of helping our crew unload equipment. Now we had to count on these inexperienced men to set up what was essentially a complex movie set. To their credit, they were extraordinarily enthusiastic and dedicated, but they needed constant guidance and supervision, and, since I was the only Spanish-speaking technician on location, the responsibility to train them fell on me. At the same time, I had to execute the required functions of the job as well as deal with all production-related problems on the set. But yet again, I was given, by the grace of God, only that which I could handle.

We were located on a remote site in a state park across the bay from Havana. At first we were working eighteen hour days so as not to fall too far behind schedule while we waited for the rest of our crew to arrive. The distances and the long hours made getting to a meeting or just getting hold of a meeting list impossible. In any event, the meetings ended long before I was done with my day's work, and the most that I was able to accomplish was to play phone tag with the contact number I'd brought with me. However, on Saturday, our third day, I talked to an AA member who suggested Grupo Havana, which met the next day at two in the afternoon.

By this point the rest of our crew had made it in from Mexico and we were caught up with some of our work. So I arranged to take my lunch break around the time of the meeting. My request was met with great curiosity.

"What personal business could you have in Havana?" I was asked by a fellow worker who perhaps suspected that I was trying to sneak in some sightseeing on the other side of the bay. I told them, "Let's just say that I know people all over."

The meeting was located in Central Havana in a classroom in one of the city's oldest churches. It was not unlike many other AA rooms which I was accustomed to in New York, except for the ceiling fans, whose sole purpose was to swirl the sultry air. And, of course, all the AA slogans were in Spanish. When I arrived, the room was full and the meeting had not quite begun. I found a seat in the first row and sat back, grateful to finally be at a meeting.

Then I noticed several men with professional videotape equipment who were congregated in the front of the room. Their equipment and their lack of suntans led me to assume that they were in the same circumstances as myself — that is, they were on assignment in Cuba and looking for a meeting. After ten minutes or so, they moved to the back of the room and the meeting got under way.

It was an anniversary meeting and a first-year celebrant proudly took his place at the podium and began to speak. Suddenly, I noticed that the camera crew had set up in a corner in the back of the room and had started to record the proceedings with their professional camera and boom mike. It was a startling sight! "This can't be happening," I thought.

I knew it was inappropriate for them to videotape the meeting. But was it appropriate for me to intervene? Speaking up when necessary is one of the things I find hardest to do. "What right do I have to protest at a meeting in a foreign country?" I asked myself.

This was now a most uncomfortable place for me. "Man, I just wanted a meeting," I whined to myself. "I don't need this!"

I didn't know what to do except what I've learned to do in moments of duress and confusion. I closed my eyes and prayed. I asked my Higher Power for guidance, strength, and courage.

In the next moment, I found myself in the back of the room talking to the film crew members. I whispered, "Excuse me, fellows. It's against the traditions of Alcoholics Anonymous to film or videotape AA meetings."

"Yes, it's okay. We are from German television. We have shot an AA meeting before, in Munich," responded a man who identified himself as the producer and correspondent. "Anyway, we are only shooting the back of their heads." Then he flashed me his press card.

"Well, right now your camera is pointed directly at the speaker's face," I said. "And that is not acceptable."

He said, "Yes, but that man gave us permission to do so."

"Be that as it may," I said, "it's still not right. Perhaps he isn't aware of all our Traditions, and that's why he agreed. If you don't show his face — if you shoot him from the neck down — that would adhere to our Traditions."

"But that's ridiculous," he protested. "It will only distract us from the story we want to tell! What is the point to shoot him from the neck down?"

"Look, I'm in the same business as you are and I sympathize with your need for accuracy in your work." I showed him my own set of television journalist's credentials. "But here in AA, we must put our Tradition of anonymity before all else. That is the point in shooting him from the neck down! And that is also why, gentlemen, I must insist that you only shoot all of us from the neck down."

"You arrogant American!" the cameraman angrily interrupted. "You think you can come down here to a foreign country and tell us how to conduct our business!"

The tropical sun and all the pressures of the last few days seized me at that moment, and I exploded. "Bull! This has nothing to do with journalism! This has to do solely with respecting one of the things that holds our vital AA program together — anonymity!"

This high-volumed exchange got everyone's attention. Embarrassed and not sure if I could maintain my composure, I suggested that we move the conversation to the hallway, and at this point, several of the group's members joined us. These Grupo Havana members, who had from four to five years of sobriety each, were old-timers by Cuban standards (Grupo Havana, the oldest meeting in Cuba, was seven years old). Armed with a Spanish-language copy of *Twelve Steps and Twelve Traditions* opened to the chapter on the Eleventh Tradition, they patiently explained to the frustrated television producer the meaning and the importance behind the principle of anonymity. These old-timers brought a certain articulation and dignity to the discussion that made me feel privileged to be part of this special Fellowship of ours.

The German producer in turn argued that our book was archaic, that it was written years ago when the conventions of the public and media were different. We explained that anonymity had been critical to our survival as a Fellowship.

"But this piece will be aired only in Germany," he went on. "No one here will see it. Your anonymity will be safe."

"That it's only shown in Germany doesn't matter. I didn't know two months ago that I'd be in Cuba today. But because of this Tradition, I can travel to virtually any civilized place on this planet and feel safe. I don't really know where my job or my heart will take me next. I could very well find myself in Munich next month!"

As the words left my mouth, I realized the answer to the question I had asked myself earlier: Who am I to intervene in another group's business? The answer is that it's my responsibility as a member of Alcoholics Anonymous to speak up whenever our common welfare is at stake.

In the end, the producer declared, "If we can only shoot from the neck down, we will leave!" And with that, they packed up their equipment and left.

During the meeting, when my turn came to share, I said, "I apologize for losing my temper. For that, I have regret. But I hold strongly to the convictions which I stand by with respect to our Traditions. There are no leaders in AA nor do we tell others how to conduct their business, but as a member, I felt compelled to say something to the television crew. This has not been easy for me. But it would have been unbearable to me to live with my own silence."

At the break, many members came up to me and offered their phone numbers, telling me to call any time of the day and that I wasn't alone in Havana. One old-timer who had participated in the discussion in the hallway kindly said to me, "Relax. We're grateful you spoke up. It is not always easy for us to do so in our country, especially when foreigners are involved. Besides, perhaps you were supposed to be here today to take the initiative for us. Here in Cuba, we AAs do not believe in coincidences."

"Neither do we in New York," I said. "We say that coincidences are merely a manner in which God protects his anonymity!"

Federico
(January 1999)

⟞⟨⬦⟩⟝

A LONG WAY FROM HOME

Moratuwa, Sri Lanka

I arrived in Alcoholics Anonymous nine years ago in Los Angeles, feeling alone and scared, too afraid to trust anyone. In the years since, I've done many things I did not expect. I have switched careers and vacationed in exotic lands. I have gained and lost money, jobs, real estate, and a marriage. I have lost more in sobriety than I ever imagined I'd have when I walked through the doors of AA. Life has not always been the way I have wanted it, but it has often been exciting, and I have been taken care of at every step. Through each triumph, crisis, and experience, I have come to value more and more the support of meetings and people in AA.

I am an agnostic. I practice a spiritual program and I believe wholeheartedly in the Twelve Steps, but I do not have a personal concept of a Higher Power that could be called God. I have come to believe that what I do is more important than what I think: I was told when I got sober that I could act my way into right thinking, but I could never think my way into right action.

The quest for a satisfying spiritual path, combined with a sudden reduction in worldly responsibilities, led me to volunteer for a year in Sri Lanka, a poor country with a rich spiritual history. Letting go of my familiar surroundings was a difficult decision for me to make, yet over a period of months I became convinced that this was the right step for me to take. "Your job now is to be at the place where you may be of maximum helpfulness to others, so never hesitate to go anywhere if you can be helpful." (Big Book, p. 102)

When the decision had been made, I sold everything except a few personal items stored in boxes in Los Angeles. The one thing I worried about giving up was my AA support group. The Big Book has kept me centered when I couldn't get to a meeting — but that was for a few days, not the twelve months I planned to be away this time! I was nervous as I made the last of the arrangements. By the time I boarded the plane for my journey halfway around the world, I was convinced I was crazy. But I had my Big Book and the International Directory, and together they gave me some solace.

I didn't know what to expect in Sri Lanka. I knew no one, and I knew nothing about the living conditions or the specific work I was expected to do; only that I would do computer work for a charity organization that promotes spiritual values, and that in return they would give me food and shelter and the opportunity to explore my spiritual path.

As it turned out, everything worked out fine. Although my accomodations are not as comfortable as what I have been accustomed to, I am well taken care of. The organization teaches a program of service and spiritual growth that sounds very familiar, though it focuses on poverty and social problems instead of alcoholism. And there are enough people who speak enough English that I am able to get my work done and carry on basic conversations.

And yet, for the first six weeks, I felt alone. Although everyone was friendly, I felt different. I looked different, of course, and was treated as an honored guest, always a bit separated from my hosts. I did not speak the language or understand the culture. And there was no one to whom I could talk about the emotional issues of sobriety: the inevitable resentments, anger, fear, and other emotions that disturb my serenity on a daily basis.

For six weeks, I wrote letters home and mailed Tenth Step inventories to my sponsor. I wrote to the local intergroup office in the town of Colombo and got a meeting directory, but the meetings were forty-five minutes away by bus, and I didn't know the area well enough to travel on my own. I was afraid to break my anonymity to anyone within my host organization in order to ask for directions.

For six weeks I worked the program alone, until I felt completely isolated from both my new coworkers and my AA friends back home.

Finally, I made a telephone call to the contact at the intergroup office. I had a lot of fear. Would he speak English? Would he laugh at my Los Angeles program? Is alcoholism the same here? Are they plagued by anger and resentment?

I needn't have worried. The man spoke very good English, and invited me to his house before the meeting, giving me precise directions on how to find it. When I arrived, he was sitting on the porch listening to another alcoholic tell about getting angry on the bus and wanting to hit someone. I was home.

The meeting was smaller than my home group, but alcoholics in Sri Lanka deal with the same issues as those in Los Angeles. They work the same Twelve Steps to maintain their spiritual health. A bonus for me is that all four of the country's major religions are represented: Buddhism, Hinduism, Christianity, and Islam. I have an opportunity to hear about this program of spiritual growth from a variety of perspectives. A meeting is still a major outing for me — forty-five minutes each way on a crowded bus — but I make it a point to go once a week. On those weeks I have skipped, I have inevitably found myself on edge — "restless, irritable, and discontented." As someone once observed, the program can be worked without direct contact with another alcoholic — but given the choice, why would one? It's so much easier when we support each other.

Another lesson I relearned is about secrets. For three months, I didn't tell anyone at the host organization where I went one evening a week. When someone asked, I said I was having dinner and visiting friends — not exactly untrue. Yet over time, I felt a barrier growing between me and my hosts, and I didn't understand why.

One day I found myself ready to explode over some insignificant event, and I had to stop and look at my behavior. I realized that I was living a secret life, very much like I did in the old days.

Whether or not it was anyone else's business, I had to confide the truth to someone, for my own sanity. I chose the person closest to me in the organization, my coordinator. His reaction was one of puzzlement, but not the condemnation I feared. He had never heard of Alcoholics Anonymous, and he seemed to think I didn't look like an alcoholic.

All religions teach some form of confession, and Buddhism is no exception. My friend understood my need to eliminate the secret, and was curious about the spiritual nature of the program. There is very little AA literature available in the Sinhala language, but I have offered him what I can find.

By introducing Alcoholics Anonymous to a member of a service organization with similar spiritual principles, perhaps I have been of service to some future alcoholic my friend may meet. In any case, I have learned once again that I can't stay sober alone, and that situations I fear are rarely as bad as the fear itself! And I found a home 12,000 miles from my home group.

D. M.
(September 1994)

New Life in Lurigancho

Macate Via Chimbote, Peru

"Bring only your passport and 15,000 *soles*," my friend had told me. "Nothing else. Don't wear a belt. The guards at the prison won't let you wear it in and then you'll never see it again."

Such were my instructions the night before our Twelfth Step call upon several incarcerated alcoholics.

Lima, Peru, is surrounded by grim, dusty barrios of adobe and straw huts that stretch on like a puzzle before one's unaccustomed eyes. From one of the better parts of town we drove through several of these bleak areas. The paved road ended and we traveled over dirt roads seemingly abandoned ten years previously in the middle of construction.

We arrived in Lurigancho, the *pueblo joven* (literally, "young town"; actually, "shantytown") where the prison taking its name from the area stands up hard against barren hills that vaguely suggest the Andes beyond. Outside, a line of visitors a half-mile long had already formed by 8:30 a.m. Nasty-looking guards strolled about, occasionally abusing a vendor or visitor who crossed them. "Here, I am in charge!" one yelled, as he pushed a woman selling juice out of his way.

During the drive from the comfortable house of my Peruvian hosts to this dusty scene of disorder, I was rather distracted by. . . yes, self-centered fear. "What if there's a mix-up and I am left inside the prison? What if some inmates kidnap me? What if there's a riot while we're inside?"

Perhaps you too have been crippled by the "what if's." But then, something from the Big Book came to mind, something along the lines of not hesitating to visit even the most sordid place on earth if you can be of service. God would be there. During those few moments when my motives are truly good, and I am sure about God's work, I always feel completely safe. (Conversely, it tells me how insecure I often am during daily life.)

"We'll never get in if we have to get on that line," my friend exclaimed. So he led me on a ritual with different guards, each of whom he addressed with great respect. One laughed and turned his back, another sent us to the back of the line. Undeterred, we approached a third, showing our documents: a letter of authorization from some official; my missionary visa from another country; a church bulletin with my friend's name on it. "A friend of Bill Wilson" was not useful status with these guards, whose brutality is such that the government does not allow them within the prison walls. Inside, unarmed civilian guards do the work.

The last guard relented and in we went, passing through three checkpoints and four locked doors. The nonviolent prisoners are kept in a separate pavilion, heavily barricaded in case of a breakout or riot by the violent prisoners. Finally, within the building holding foreign nationals, we spotted our man on the other side of the barred door. He came forth to greet us, smiling. I was stunned. Imagine, smiling in such a place. Behind him, a scene from the Inferno appeared — anarchy in an open cell block. People were everywhere, doing everything. And there stood "Ken," sober and happy.

Once inside, we sat down at a rough wooden table with three men, two Americans and one European. They secured some eggs, bread, and coffee for us from a vendor. The prison has a thriving cash economy for food, medicine, clothing, bedding, drugs, and alcohol as well. One needs money to survive. Left to the meager provisions of the authorities, one can suffer illness and malnutrition.

"We've been sober for a week," Ken and the other American told us. It seemed a most impressive accomplishment. The third man was also sober, but he did not say for how long. The three of them had that light in their eyes and joy on their faces that we see in those who delight in their sobriety. I had little to say, I was so absorbed. Ken spoke of how "We had been reading the Bible recently, and were at the section, in Mark I think, where it says something about 'when you visited those in prison, you visited me.'" His friend interrupted, "Well, actually it said, 'when you came unto me in prison,' and there is a big difference between 'coming unto' and just 'visiting.'"

The citation may not have been right, and the quotation paraphrased, but never have those words been so alive for me. It was a moment when familiar words were suddenly fraught with a new and fuller meaning, a meaning beyond words. I was overcome with emotion, with gratitude, with enlightenment. Our friends there in Lurigancho thought we had done them a favor, while I felt myself to be quite the recipient. Familiar words were given new life.

"We've been sober for a week." Those words meant that a miracle had taken place. Yes, it is always a miracle, but during my first week of sobriety I had endless meetings and new friends to help me. There was a place I called home, encouragement from family and friends, and the liberty to remove myself from disturbing influences. These three recovering alcoholics were holding on in one of the worst prisons in the free world.

"We've been sober for a week." The words told us, "Yes, we're in a hellhole, but we're not drinking and we're happy about it." Sometimes we just have to hear the words in a certain situation for the deeper significance to hit us. Other times the words coming out of our own mouths mean more given the circumstances.

Earlier this year, I studied Spanish in Quito, Ecuador, for six weeks. The AA meetings I attended there could have been in Russian for all that I understood. Yet the sentiment was clear. It was the sentiment, the consensus that fires every meeting: "We are alcoholics who want to live." Once, I did understand a man who was shouting rhetorically, "We understand the alcoholic. . . ." Isn't that the basic message of every meeting? At my first meetings, I had a strong reaction to something foreign in the air. These people understood me! While I was drinking, friends, family, girlfriends had all offered advice, suggestions, pity, bewilderment, vague and often misplaced hope, but they did not, they could not understand. They were not recovering alcoholics. The words "we understand" gave me another chance to live.

Every meeting, every encounter with another member of Alcoholics Anonymous offers that blessed opportunity to be with someone who understands. And my presence announces that I want to live, rather than die from drinking. On both sides, I can grow complacent and forget the message behind the words. My friend in Quito had to shout, repeatedly, "We understand," for me to remember thankfully, "Yes, they do." The words are at every meeting. Because someone understands, I do not have to die. Because someone will listen, I can live.

I can tell my story though, or parts of it, with little feeling, the words just coming forth, barely beckoned. Words are then like little objects I toss out toward others as a matter of protocol. "My first drink was at my sister's wedding . . . I came to AA when I was about to die . . . nowhere else to go." Yawn. "Well," I think, "I am at a meeting. I should be saying these things."

Several weeks in Quito had passed. I sat mutely through four meetings, and the only real encounters with other alcoholics were through the mail. Desperate action was called for. I waylaid a man after a meeting and conveyed my need to talk. We made a date, met, and after pleasantries he asked, "Porque te unistes Alcohólicos Anónimos?" (Why did you join Alcoholics Anonymous?)

Over a million AAs in 114 countries reached out to me in that question. Every meeting asks that question, my every attendance answers it. Rarely have I answered with such feeling, such eagerness. Rarely have the words of the query been so pregnant with invitation, hope, help, promise. In the words of my reply I explain myself and save my life. That afternoon, in a forty-five-minute torrent of broken Spanish, I did just that. Words, at other times tired and stale, had life.

There are days when I look forlornly back on my past, and contemplate the "young man of promise" whose brilliant career I imagine to have been arbitrarily derailed by alcoholism. The great dreams have been drearily replaced by a colorless struggle not to pick up the next drink. At the end of such days, I sadly conclude, "All I did today was not drink." But then it can grip me, "I did not drink!" And the words can come alive with the miles of meaning behind them. "I am sober! I am alive! And I almost died from drinking."

Last month, I endured an eleven-hour truck ride, sitting on a plank, along a dirt road down from the Andean village I live in, to the nearest city, 9,000 feet below on the coast. The scenery lost its charm, and as we stopped for the fifth time to strap the suspension springs together with rope and logs, I could only think, "How boring. How pointless." Then I recalled the utter boredom of daily life back in the dark ages, and how I drank to fend off life. Morosely I consoled myself, "But I'm sober." Then, great awareness of the miracle galvanized me. "Yes! I'm sober. I haven't had a drink today." I looked at my fellow dust-covered weary passengers sitting around me. "How about that!" I thought.

C. R.
(July 1986)

————◦⦿◦————

THE DAWN OF A NEW DAY

Mexico City, Mexico

While I was on the AA state committee, I received a call from Sister Alicia in the town of Santa Maria Alotepec Mixe. Her parish served the Mixe people. She had heard about AA in Mexico City and decided to ask for our help. She told me the problem of alcoholism was a desperate one in the entire region. She wanted us to bring AA to the Mixes. When I heard her story, my immediate response was: "Of course we'll go."

The Mixes live in the northern region of Mexico, in the state of Oaxaca. Some scholars believe that they originated in the tropical region of the Gulf of Mexico, while others believe that the Mixes emigrated from Peru. The Mixes arrived in Oaxaca seeking Zempoalteped, "the Hill of the Twenty Divinities." Neither the Zapotecs, Mixtecs, or Aztecs were ever able to conquer them. The Spaniards defeated them but not before tasting the bravery of the Mixe warriors. In 1970, the Mixe population consisted of about 79,000 people spread out over 19 municipalities and 106 communities.

Sister Alicia explained that the trip would be a long, difficult one. "The journey to Ayutla Mixe," she told me, "takes four hours by vehicle — preferably a pickup truck. There you will find two men who will act as guides. The pickup can take you on to Cacalotepec, but from there you'll have to walk for ten hours." I thought, "Anyone can walk ten hours." I imagined walking down lanes bordered with wildflowers, breathing the air of the forest, and admiring the scenic wilderness.

So, at six o'clock on a Tuesday morning, our band of eight men and women and two children set out in a borrowed station wagon. At Ayutla we met with our guides and from there, two of us walked with the pack animals, following the station wagon. Night had fallen by the time we reached a place called Vistahermosa, and we stopped and slept a few hours before starting out at four the next morning.

At ten the next day we arrived at the town of Cacalotepec. But we had troubles: One of our group was suffering from painfully swollen knees and another had twisted his ankle. Our guides told us they didn't want to take people who were hurt. Over breakfast we discussed the situation and decided to slim down the group. Five people went back — including the two children — while five of us continued toward our next stop, Morelos Ranch.

We walked on what seemed an interminable track on a constant rise toward the mountains, step by step, one after the other. I frequently recalled the words of Sister Alicia: "You'll have to walk ten hours," and kept repeating that to myself, for encouragement. Slowly we progressed, in spite of our extreme tiredness and the sun's burning heat. At last we descended toward Morelos Ranch, a cheerful little town in a semitropical climate, located at the edge of a stream. After a brief but refreshing rest, we started up again. I was beginning to wonder about Sister Alicia's "ten hours."

Due to my exhaustion, one of the guides — named Reynaldo — almost always walked by my side. Reynaldo was Mixe by origin and birth, but had lived in the cities of Chiapas and Oaxaca. He and his family had been forced by circumstances to learn Spanish, and because he was bilingual, he later became our translator and interpreter.

Walking along with Reynaldo gave me a chance to speak to him about the AA program. As is common for people who aren't familiar with AA, Reynaldo was on the defensive. He was not, he told me, an alcoholic. He said he drank when he wanted to and that when he didn't want to, he stopped. Willpower was all that was needed.

We were now headed toward the Mixe mountain range. Tiredness was heavy upon us. Then Reynaldo — out of I don't know where — brought forth a bottle of *mescal* (a liquor which has a very high alcohol content). With a mock serious grin, he said, "This takes away tiredness." I sat down at the edge of the path and watched him take a few large swigs of good *mescal*. He laughed while waiting for me to say something. "Yes," I said, "it does remove tiredness. Let me have a little." And I raised my trouser cuffs and rubbed some *mescal* on my ankles.

We made camp that night in the dark at a place called Cortamonte. The guides made coffee and we ate dinner around the fire amid laughter and amusing comments. Our bodies were tired but at no time did our spirits flag. We then prepared our country beds. How lovely it was to sleep in the mountains, watching the stars at night and feeling very close to our Higher Power. We were all silent when suddenly we heard the roar of a beast. In alarm, someone asked, "What was that?" One of the guides said, "It's a small panther. Do not be afraid — it is some distance away and will not approach our fire." As for me, I was, so tired that I promptly fell asleep.

At four o'clock in the morning we were on our way, once again climbing and climbing. This was the last stage of our journey. At daybreak we spotted a small chapel and beyond it the town of Santa Maria Alotepec Mixe — at last! We would soon be there. I stopped for a few moments at the chapel to rest and thank God for allowing us to arrive.

In town, Sister Alicia, Father Leopoldo, and three other sisters greeted us warmly. We breakfasted, and after a rest, a good rubbing of alcohol (on the outside!), we met for the first time with some of the townspeople, in a small room lent to us.

In this meeting, as in all others, Reynaldo was our translator. In the morning, we decided to have a public information meeting. In the afternoon, we had a "therapy session" and explained what the AA recovery program consisted of. That night as we prepared to retire, we made hopeful comments among ourselves. We had noted the enthusiasm of our guide Reynaldo as we spoke in Spanish and he translated into the Mixe language. We were almost sure that some of his fellow countrymen were interested. We were optimistic.

On the next day we held two more meetings. We explained to the Mixes that we formed AA groups in order to keep our sobriety and save our own lives. We spoke a little about the Traditions, especially the First Tradition, which stresses the importance of our common welfare. We also spoke of the right every human being has to stop suffering by quitting drinking.

We left the little meeting room, giving the Mixes freedom to choose. They alone, led by Reynaldo, created their groups. So, now there were nineteen new members of AA! They decided their meeting days would be Saturdays and Sundays. Seeds were planted that would germinate in very short order.

On Saturday we prepared to return to Oaxaca. Now it was time for Reynaldo to say good-bye. Tears were streaming down his face. "Brothers, forgive me," he said. "I did not want you to come to my village! That is why I brought you on the long, most difficult way. Forgive me, because I am an alcoholic!"

In honor of the difficult path which had brought us there, I suggested to my friends that the new group be called Meeg Tuu, which in the Mixe language means "virtuous path." And so it was that the first AA group of the Mixes was born in Santa Maria Alotepec Mixe, in the spring of 1978.

The following year, on the first anniversary of the Meeg Tuu Group, a way was found to establish three additional groups: the Stairs of Stone Group in San Pedrito Ayacaxtepec Mixe, the San Jose Group in Ayutla Mixe, and the Sons of Kondoy Group in Yokachi-Mixe. Two more groups were established later that year: the Mouth of the Mountain Group and the New Generation Group. Today, there are more groups in Chuxnaban, in Cotzocan, in Cacalotepec, and in Morelos Ranch.

All of this happened by the grace of God, and the plea of Sister Alicia: "Will you carry the AA message to the Mixes?"

Miguel O.
(September 1992)

'They Had What I Wanted'

West Wyalong, New South Wales, Australia

My name is Bill and I'm an alcoholic. I'm also an Aboriginal Australian — a Koori. I got sober twenty-eight years ago in western New South Wales. I was desperate; I was at what the Big Book refers to as "the jumping-off place." The book was written many years ago, but these words still express the point I had reached: "He cannot picture life without alcohol. Some day he will be unable to imagine life either with alcohol or without it. Then he will know loneliness such as few do. He will be at the jumping-off place. He will wish for the end."

Those words describe the rock-bottom despair of alcoholism as experienced by a group of white male American alcoholics, but no matter if you're black or white, male or female, young or old, in jail or out of jail, if you're an alcoholic, sooner or later you'll reach that point.

In Australia, however, because of cultural differences, it can be difficult for an Aboriginal Australian to identify with white speakers in an AA meeting, no matter how parallel their drinking stories may be. For instance, I heard one white speaker at a meeting say, "It got so bad that I ended up drinking down on the riverbank with some Abos!" Well, that's where my drinking began and I ended up even further downhill — drinking with some white blokes in Melbourne. Now, there's a really low rock-bottom for you! I mention this only to illustrate that, despite AA being a very easy-going and tolerant outfit, thoughtless remarks can occur in meetings from time to time which inhibit the kind of identification that is central to the AA process.

Another problem that Aboriginal alcoholics face comes from the downtrodden history of our people. Now that we are starting to rediscover and take pride in our culture, it is only natural for some Kooris to dismiss anything "white," including "white medicine," as being alien. Many of my people, concerned with the damage done by "grog" to the Kooris, have looked for an Aboriginal "cure" for alcoholism or have tried to "Aboriginalize" AA before offering it to native Australians.

Such efforts can be worthwhile; however, we would be remiss in our efforts if we didn't first look at the mistakes made by those who brought AA to Australia in the nineteen-forties. Some of them thought they first needed to modify the "American" AA program before applying it to Australian drunks. Unfortunately, many drank again and died. "Modified" AA didn't seem to produce too many lasting recoveries. Penicillin doesn't need to be "Australianized" or "Aboriginalized" before it will work on a Koori with pneumonia. Neither does the AA program need to be "Aboriginalized" before it will work with native Australians suffering from the illness of alcoholism. Quite a few Koori alcoholics, and I'm one of them, have gotten sober and stayed sober in mixed AA meetings.

Recently, we had a "Royal Commission" (government investigation) to look into the problem of Aboriginal deaths in custody. The inquiry was sparked by the high rate of arrest, imprisonment, and deaths in custody of Aboriginal people throughout Australia. During the investigation, a statistician assisting the Commission made public some figures showing a much higher ratio of Aboriginals being arrested than whites, mainly for drink-related offenses. However, once they were in custody, the statistician reported that Kooris and whites were dying, mostly from suicide, at about the same distressing rate. That news hit like a bombshell and the brave statistician was criticized by many Kooris since his figures went right up against the basic assumption underlying all the Royal Commission's work, that there was either something inherent in the Aboriginal psyche that was leading to the suicides or that they were the result of the treatment received by the white authorities. Nobody up until then had realized that there was an equally high rate of suicides for white prisoners in custody.

When I read those statistics, I had a moment of understanding and I thought, "They're not dying because they're Aboriginals. They're necking themselves because they're alcoholics who can't get a drink to ease the pain. And the white guys are doing the same. I've been there. I've felt like that myself."

Many alcoholics, black and white, are in custody today for issues related to drinking and are suffering from alcohol withdrawal. They're in a bad way, physically and mentally. Many are in total denial about being alcoholics but are also in total despair about their future. They are at "the jumping-off place."

Fortunately we now know there is a solution, that such drastic hopelessness can be changed, and changed quite dramatically — by joining or forming local AA groups and by putting AA principles into practice. There are now more than two million alcoholics worldwide who have recovered from that "seemingly hopeless state of mind and body." They're still alcoholics but they're sober and they've recovered from what is also described in the Big Book as "pitiful and incomprehensible demoralization."

In 1968, it took what was left of my courage to stand up at a small-town AA meeting and identify myself as an alcoholic. I listened to the stories and I identified. By joining in with those AA members and doing what they were doing, I haven't touched a drop from that day to this. So, for all those Kooris drinking their lives away in town parks and outback camps around Australia, I say that there is now another way out of the misery apart from the bottle or suicide, and that is AA.

There are a number of meetings now in Australia for Kooris run by Kooris. These can remove some of the stumbling blocks new Koori members might face when they first approach AA. But for those Kooris who are looking to get off and stay off the booze and may not have a special-purpose Koori meeting nearby, they'll need the courage to do as I did and stand up at a mixed meeting and ask for help. I'm just as committed to Aboriginal culture as my fellow Kooris, but I'm also committed to staying sober the AA way, simply because it works. Being sober in AA has enabled me to participate in all kinds of community and family activities. These had been taken from me or denied me, not by white Australia but by the disease of alcoholism.

Luckily for me, at my first AA meeting I was too sick to notice anything other than the drunks there with stories just as bad as mine. They'd all been terrible drunks, hopeless alcoholics, but they were no longer drinking and they had hope. They were sober and getting on with life. Some had been sober for many years and they were happy about it. I wanted what they had and I set about getting it.

Bill R.
(March 1997)

A Red-Letter Day

Kingston, Jamaica

It was to be a special day for the King Street AA in Spanish Town. Derrick, our first new member, was due to receive his three-month medallion, and our second new member, Ramon, was here for his first meeting. It had been a long haul. For almost four months, we had made the weekly trip from Kingston to Spanish Town, apparently for no good purpose. We wanted to start a new group there, but why travel all that way just to talk to ourselves? It seemed that, after all, we were only carrying the message to those who had it already. But today, at last, it began to seem worthwhile. This is how we arrived at that red letter day.

We had thought that Jamaica finally had a solid base in AA. A group in Montego Bay met three times a week and there were a few members as well in Ocho Rios — so at least the tourists on the north coast could find a home away from home. In Kingston, on the other end of the island, we had meetings six days a week, and in our Liguanea groups sometimes there were twenty-five or thirty at a meeting. True, most of our old-timers are themselves not so old in the program. You can count on the fingers of one hand those whose years of sobriety are in double figures — and you will have fingers to spare, at that! The rest of us? Those of us with three years' sobriety thought we really could teach all those youngsters in the program a thing or two.

That's when our group conscience at Liguanea AA decided that we needed a "carry the message committee." Maybe that was passing the buck, because the Fifth Tradition does say that "carrying the message" is the primary purpose of the whole group — not just of a committee. So we might have been wrong in shunting this responsibility off to just a few members. Still, "it works if you work it." The committee didn't last very long; nobody is quite sure now whether or not it still exists. But while it survived, it did accomplish two very important things.

First, the group spent the princely sum of four dollars U.S. (twenty-two Jamaican dollars) for a batch of responsibility cards to leave on our pamphlet rack. Now the entire group (not just the committee) is forever reminded: "I am responsible. When anyone, anywhere, reaches out for help, I want the hand of AA always to be there. And for that: I am responsible."

Second, we began to wonder if as a group we were really serious about carrying the message. Here we were placidly doing our own thing on opposite ends of the island while we knew quite well that out there in the middle of the island were all those others who so desperately needed what we already had.

So, we determined to spread our wings a bit — to begin, at least to the extent that we could help it, a gradual expansion of AA into the country parts of Jamaica. Pointing in both directions from Kingston — east and west — we would first concentrate on Harbour View to the east and Spanish Town to the west. A few members for each place would commit themselves to find a location there for meetings and to travel out each week for at least a period of one year in the hope of attracting new members who might find it difficult to get into the city for meetings.

Dorothy, David, and Moe were the members who committed themselves to Spanish Town. It wasn't hard to find the location. The pastor of the church at King Street gave us a hearty welcome. He had a few benches and tables in a roof-covered spot in the churchyard which seemed ideal. With high hopes, we christened it the "King Street AA" rather than the "Spanish Town AA." Obviously, this was going to be only the first of many new Spanish Town AA groups!

Then, for months, we began the sometimes discouraging process of carrying the message to ourselves. Sometimes a few other members from our Liguanea Group or another Kingston group would join us, but too often it turned out to be just Dorothy and David, Moe and Dorothy, or David and Moe. The biggest number we got for months was seven — and all were Kingston people. What was the sense of it all? Why not just stay in Kingston and run the meetings there?

Then came Derrick! That day we shifted to Step One for his benefit; we introduced him to the Big Book and some of the other literature. But all fingers were crossed. Derrick was not from Spanish Town; in fact, he had to take three separate country buses from the interior of the island to get to the meetings. So we waited with some anxiety to see whether or not he would show up again. But there he was the next week, all filled with enthusiasm about what had been happening to him. Maybe it was going to be worthwhile, after all.

Then came the red letter day. It was Derrick's time for his three-month medallion. With another new member there — Ramon — we shifted again to a discussion of Step One. Dorothy paused after introducing the Step and then it came: "I'm Derrick, and I'm an alcoholic," said our 90-day wonder. And with that, he turned to Ramon and began to tell him what AA does for the alcoholic.

"Out of the mouths of babes. . ." Sometimes we hear it said at meetings that a newcomer should say nothing and just listen for six months or a year into the program. Nobody could possibly defend that dogma who had the chance to hear Derrick that afternoon as he told Ramon what it is all about. All of us have been at meetings when something is said by a member which really touches the heart — when even the most hard-boiled member furtively brushes at his eyes, hoping that nobody notices. Derrick's explanation of the program that day to Ramon was surely one of those moments. "Lord, what I would have given for a tape recorder!" Dorothy said as we headed back to Kingston (and we all found that the road from Spanish Town to Kingston was blurred with a bit of mist on our return trip).

Yes, it works if you work it. Finally, we weren't just talking to ourselves any longer. That "carry the message committee," mistaken or not, was finally working.

And the new group trying to get a start at Harbour View in the other direction from Kingston? The members committed to that fledgling new group are still carrying the message to themselves alone. Is it worthwhile? You bet your sweet life it is! Just ask Dorothy, or David, or Moe — or better still, ask Derrick or Ramon.

M. W.
(July 1990)

ECHOES AROUND THE WORLD

Daytona Beach, Florida

Not long ago, I sat at a meeting in the club and thought, "Every hour around the clock, around the world, someone somewhere is opening a group meeting with our Preamble." I was inspired to a feeling of humble gratitude for being allowed to be a part of the most significant Fellowship in all the world.

"You have friends all over the world." That was J. M., in Glasgow, Scotland, telling me of a Fellowship with a range that I could not conceive at the time.

Since then, I have learned of what happened to D.C., an English-speaking AA in serious trouble in Barcelona, Spain. There, he was twelfth-stepped by members of an English-speaking group from Madrid. They had traveled many miles, in three cars, to be at his side sharing their strength when he needed it, to help him save his many years of sobriety.

Other examples — less spectacular, maybe, but just as spiritual — are my own experiences on both sides of the Atlantic. No matter where I went in Great Britain, wherever there was an AA sign, I was given openhearted friendship, just as I have been given in Titusville, Orlando, Fort Lauderdale, and Pompano, in Manhattan and Brooklyn, U.S.A. In those communities and many others, I learned that the Scotsman wasn't exaggerating; we do have loving, warm friends all over the world.

Is it any wonder that I am overwhelmed with childlike awe and with gratitude when I hear our Preamble? "Alcoholics Anonymous is a fellowship of men and women. . . ." What infinite treasure is in that description for me — compassion, love, and understanding from hundreds, thousands, a million. It's incredible!

". . . who share their experience, strength and hope . . ." Did you hear that magical word "hope"? I did. I had thought there was none for me. No one had ever offered me such priceless gifts: your strength and hope when I had none; your experience in achieving sobriety and in holding on to it one day at a time. You believed in me, when I didn't.

". . . that they may solve their common problem and help others to recover from alcoholism." It was immediately obvious to me that AA was working for you. Your faces were filled with happiness in being alive; in your eyes, you showed sobriety and the joy of living. You turned your attention to me, freely offering me help to recover and learn how to get what you had.

"The only requirement for membership is a desire to stop drinking." I could hardly believe it. Whether I was a man or a woman, black or white, rich or poor, young or old, English-speaking or otherwise, all that was inconsequential. You beautiful people offered your hand with no prejudice, no suspicions about who I was, where I came from, or what I'd done.

I had no funds nor the promise of any. You told me, "There are no dues or fees for AA membership." You said I had paid my "dues" before I got here. Every obstacle was removed from your threshold to hope.

What rich philanthropist or benefactor had kept your doors open until then? How was it possible that such a lifesaving group could exist? You told me, "We are self-supporting through our own contributions." Thank God, in your own recovery, you didn't forget its source; you showed generous, sober support of your group. If it hadn't been for that, you couldn't have been there to save my life.

"AA is not allied with any sect, denomination, politics, organization, or institution. . . ." I didn't have to be politically inclined or even aware of who was running the government. Nor did it matter that I wasn't Christian, Jewish, or Muslim, or had no religious experience at all. You made me welcome with the assurance that with the higher power of AA and an open mind, I could find a God of my own understanding and a spiritual life of my own. Thank you for your unlimited compassion, tolerance, and understanding. Today, I have found my own Higher Power through you.

". . . does not wish to engage in any controversy, neither endorses nor opposes any causes." That statement sounded very determined and singleminded. "What, then, is your purpose?" I asked. That was made crystal clear: "Our primary purpose is to stay sober and help other alcoholics [like me] to achieve sobriety." May I never forget that!

"You have friends all over the world," I was told by an AA who just happened to be a Scot in Scotland. From so many AAs throughout the world, I have heard the same inspiring sentiment: "You are no longer alone." Each time I hear the Preamble, I recall that truth, sensing its spirit as it is echoed in over one hundred nations around the earth, in a multitude of languages.

S. R.
(March 1982)

Part Two

What We Were Like

Suddenly Something Happened

Barcelona, Spain

Perhaps those who know just a little about AA think our meetings must become dull and monotonous and our talks collapse into tiresome laments or tortured remembrances. It might seem that once we have left behind the hell we existed in, we shouldn't have to go so assiduously to these meetings, for no new thoughts or experiences are to be found there.

Not so!

As AAs, we need these lifesaving contacts to support and maintain our happily found sobriety. We need to see each other regularly, help one another with continuing problems, share them, and share too our personal triumphs and mutually enjoy them. United, we continue to walk together along the upward-winding road we took when we left drinking behind. For us, our meetings are eternally new, each offering something — whether happy or tragic — to encourage, sustain, and reaffirm our precious sobriety.

I discovered at an AA meeting that a simple recitation of the Lord's Prayer could become not the serene and humble supplication to God we are familiar with but an agonized cry of impotence, the cry of a soul hoping with every word for the miracle of liberation and salvation. The meeting had concluded, and we were ready for the final prayer. We had formed our circle, grasping each other's hands. But before anyone had said a word, Enrique asked, "Would you let me lead the prayer?"

His voice was almost a whisper, eager yet timid. He looked around the circle, waiting for our response. Enrique was like a battered little old bird spreading his shaking wings. He had a four-day beard; his tattered clothes hung loosely on his skinny frame; his dirty, ragged coat and pants were beyond patching; unwashed elbows stuck out of his sleeves. His eyes were reddened; patches of dirt obscured his face; a streak of the dirt and dried blood ran from his temple to his wrinkled cheek, changing his thin, bony face into a grotesque mask.

Enrique had visited our group before, though never exactly drunk.

Some remnant of innate dignity and pride kept him from exhibiting himself as a totally destroyed person. And I had watched his unflagging battle against slavery to alcohol. Now his look was imploring us to say yes.

To his request, someone said, "Of course, Enrique. You lead the prayer tonight." Swallowing hard, Enrique prepared to lead the prayer. His eyes shut tightly, he tightened his grip on the hands of those at each side of him. His face took on a look of great intensity; sweat started out on his forehead, and he braced himself.

"Our Father who art . . ." (his voice trembling) ". . . in heaven . . ." (looking up for inspiration, for dim words in the dark tunnel of memory) "Thy kingdom come . . ." (tightened, grim mouth) ". . . thy will be done . . . " (angry, bitter rebellion against his own helplessness; tears starting down his bearded cheeks) " . . . on earth . . ." (the voice breaking now, tight in his throat) " . . . as it is in heaven . . ." (the end barely audible).

Then Enrique burst into tears and cried like a child.

No one said a word. We could not. But all of our hands gripped tighter and warmer. Everyone gazed at Enrique with compassion, love, and understanding. We identified with him. We were together with him in his defeat, for Enrique was nothing other than a repetition of our own experiences. There came the overwhelming realization that, in the fight against the ravages of alcohol, we are all truly brothers and sisters.

A. S. R.
(April 1976)

The Big Book Is About Me

Londonderry, Northern Ireland

ometimes, the question arises: "What is the Big Book really about?" With the usual alcoholic contrariness, I can only answer with a question: "Who is the Big Book about?" In dealing with alcoholism and the program of recovery, the book tells us how the first AAs dealt with the major problems engendered by our disease, problems affecting marriage, family, sex, finance, jobs, careers, and finally sanity. Through the Twelve Steps, AAs were enabled to find a new perspective on those areas of self-imposed conflict.

For me, it was simply a question of living or dying. In the course of coming to terms with these problems — in other words, coming to terms with myself — I didn't become a marriage counselor, a financial consultant, an efficiency expert, or a psychiatrist. These fields are quite rightly occupied by trained, experienced, and responsible people who must conform to socially acceptable standards before they can practice. The Big Book tells me, an alcoholic, how I can use the Twelve Steps to cope with my problems and discover who I am. The Third Step gave me a perspective from outside myself, an objective viewpoint from which I could see myself as I am, not as I would like to be, and thus helped me to approach what is now the excitement of living.

I am reminded of Thompson's "Hound of Heaven": "I fled Him, down the nights and down the days. . . . " He had to chase me, because I was running away fast. I'm thankful that I stopped running in time, long enough to read the Big Book and begin to understand it.

The Big Book is not about social, mental, or medical problems. To my question "Who is the Big Book about?" there is only one answer. The Big Book is about me.

C. F.
(May 1978)

The Streets of Bombay

Mumbai, India

The suffering of an alcoholic is not only the suffering of an individual but of all those related to him, especially those in his immediate family.

The habit of drinking small quantities every day became a necessity for me and progressed to heavy drinking. When my salary was inadequate to pay my liquor bills, I turned to loans at abnormal rates of interest. I even resigned my permanent job. After a series of blackouts, delirium tremens, and hallucinations, I met with an accident that dislocated my spine. I was treated in an orthopedic hospital for fourteen long months and was discharged with a pair of crutches. The pain and torture from this accident should have been an indelible warning for me to stay away from alcohol forever. But I took that first drink again after a lapse of almost fifteen months, only to go on a severe nonstop binge.

I pawned or sold not only my wife's ornaments but also our clothes and utensils down to the last bit. Thereafter I resorted to begging on the streets. My innocent children who could hardly get a mouthful to eat were going to school at seven a.m. with only a cup of tap water for their breakfast. In the midst of these sufferings, I could see my wife shedding tears, my children starving, our valuables sold, and the house empty. Beaten financially, physically, mentally, and spiritually, I was unable to move out of the four walls of my room.

Finding myself powerless to overcome the obsession for a drink, I preferred to commit suicide, but I had neither the strength to hold a sharp instrument in my trembling hands nor the ability to jump underneath a moving train. Finally, I lifted my eyes to the sky and cried out in despair, asking God to please let me live like a human or let me die. The very next day this God of love, compassion, and mercy, from whom I had drifted away for years, answered my prayers. He sent a messenger to my bedside with an introductory pamphlet and a request to try Alcoholics Anonymous.

The joy, love, and relief I got in my first AA meeting will remain ever fresh in my life. Listening to the sharings of my AA brethren, I was convinced that I was suffering from an incurable illness called alcoholism. God inspired me to stick to the AA members and I continued to attend regular meetings. A miracle happened. I am now living a happy contented life without the intake of alcohol for a little over twenty-one years. If I had died years ago on the Bombay streets, that indelible phrase, "Marcel died drinking," would have disturbed my wife and grown children (including a priest) even now; whereas if I died today, people would proudly and unhesitatingly comment that I died a sober death.

During my active alcoholism I had sold myself body and soul for naught, but God in his infinite mercy redeemed me through AA, free of charge. If I fail to share this free gift with my other suffering brethren there is every possibility of losing it.

I appeal to all mothers, wives, and sisters: if the disease of alcoholism has afflicted your sons, husbands, or brothers, there is hope through AA. AA is open to all, irrespective of caste, creed, and religion. Thousands of recovering alcoholics in over one hundred countries owe their lives to AA and its members. Our debt of gratitude knows no bounds.

Marcel P.
(January 1999)

———•◉•———

'THE BEST OF MY ABILITY'

Bangkok, Thailand

I am a native of Bournemouth on the south coast of England in the British Isles, but I was born nine years ago in Bangkok, Thailand on the day I found and joined the Fellowship of Alcoholics Anonymous. On that day in June, a drunken habit pattern reached a crossroads and had the opportunity to change to a sober habit pattern.

Man's life is made up of a system of habit patterns. If he wants to be an engineer, he studies, and information on engineering is stored in his memory. Eventually, that stored information is translated into a habit.

I was a very good student of alcoholism. I studied for twenty-four years. My habit patterns became totally based on how to continue drinking day in and day out. I became a past master of denial, an artist with self-pity, and by the time I heard the thumping of dirt and pebbles as they would soon be shoveled onto the lid of my coffin, the habit patterns had become permanent and I couldn't stop drinking even when I wanted to.

Such is the place that some of us find ourselves in when we join the Fellowship of AA — completely enveloped in alcoholism, mentally, spiritually, and physically.

At first, I was like a lot of others on a pink cloud for two or three weeks. Then all of a sudden, I came crashing down to earth and began to feel that awful, apprehensive, depressive pain that said if I wanted to stay stopped, I would have to change. Thank goodness, I was told at meetings that I could now live one day at time. I didn't need to project the future or cry about the past. Just live to the best of my ability, one day at a time.

I think the key in my sobriety has been the use of the concept "to the best of my ability" rather than the concept used during my active alcoholism when my abilities were required to be perfect. Even though I have family problems and I am deeply in debt because business is bad, I am a wonderfully happy, laughing person. By living the AA way of life and practicing the principles in all my affairs, I have established a new habit pattern over the past nine years. I am now continuing to get sober one day at a time, to the best of my ability.

Anonymous
(October 1988)

———◦◦◦———

PEOPLE, PLACES, AND THINGS

Kathmandu, Nepal

I was born in a small, beautiful village in the hills of Nepal. However, it was in Kathmandu, the capital city, that I took my first drink with some friends from school. My companions, I am sure, did not want me to turn into an alcoholic; they just wanted to see me enjoy life. I did not refuse the request of my friends and took several sips on their behalf. In the course of time, however, I started drinking for myself. I started spending money from my own pocket and became a regular drinker. From then on I started to spend my life as an alcoholic.

Back at home, my family somehow knew about my change of behavior and, as a result, the financial assistance given for my studies was stopped. Then I had a very hard time finding my food twice a day. With the worry of not getting money I intensified my drinking habit to forget the sorrow. By that time, the friends who used to be very close to me left this "moneyless alcoholic" alone. During the same period I was affiliated with a strong political party, but my friends within the party also started hating me as they could not persuade me to stop drinking. Finally, I had to give up the hope of their help also.

According to Nepalese culture, alcohol is strictly prohibited in the Brahmin society, and becoming desperate, I returned home. I started to control my drinking, but gradually all restraint began to fall away, and the time came when my family had to stop giving me anything except two meals a day. I was compelled to sell everything I could get my hands on in order to get a drink. Grains and cooking utensils were the easy articles. Later my family started to lock everything up. Viewing the dark future of my family, one of my relatives forced me to transfer ownership of my property to my children.

My body used to desire alcohol twenty-four hours a day. Shivering of hands and legs, unclear vision, imbalance of the body, and headaches were the usual characteristics when I didn't drink. In the morning, I had to hold one hand with the other till I could get several glasses of liquor down my throat. Finally my wife and kids could not stand it anymore and took refuge in her father's house.

Once my family left me, I was free to do anything I wanted. The first thing I did was to sell off any remaining household articles. When that was done, I started selling standing crops at far below their market value just to have some money in my hands. When there were no more crops to sell, I started detaching wood from my house. I did not even leave windows and doors. Once I tried to take out the wooden column on which the whole house was supported. Fortunately, I was unsuccessful in that endeavor. Exploiting the situation, my neighbors were only too happy to buy whatever I happened to be selling — always well below its worth.

One night I woke up needing a drink. I started out toward a *Raxi Pasal* (a shop that sells alcohol), but it was so dark that I fell down and broke my right arm. My neighbor helped me to the hospital where I spent three weeks. Several months later when I was coming out from another *Raxi Pasal*, I was so drunk that I could not control myself and slipped on the ground. This time my left arm was fractured. Again I had to spend three weeks in the hospital. While I was coming out from the hospital, the doctor who was attending me advised me to live "on the will of God, not on my own will." These words had a deep influence on my heart but I started drinking again. Within several months, as a result of my drinking, I lost two front teeth and fractured my backbone. I had to replace the teeth and undergo surgery for my back. There were also numerous events where I was beaten by the shopkeeper for not paying the money I owed after drinking. This is the way I spent half my life.

Day by day, my soul, body, and brain were diverted more toward alcohol. However, I had some feelings in a remote corner of my heart that I should give up alcohol. I thought about suicide, but I remembered one of my friends saying, "Our body is a temple of God; to destroy it is a sin." With this message I am still alive.

After spending twenty-five years with alcohol, I experienced a significant turning point in my life. A foreigner introduced me to AA. I started attending AA meetings regularly in Kathmandu. After staying sober for a little while, one day I met one of my old drinking friends. We visited a restaurant together where he took a glass of alcohol and I took a cup of tea. After having several drinks, my friend requested me to have one too, and finally I accepted his offer. After seven days of continuous drinking, I returned to my foreign friend. Though he was disappointed that I drank, he was glad to see me again. After three and a half months, the same story repeated once again. This time the door of my friend's house was closed to me. Being desperate, that night I prayed for God to show me the way. From that day onward I started to follow the lesson of staying stopped one day at a time. I started learning that the first glass is poison for me. The Twelve Steps of AA are now the backbone of my success.

It is already more than a year, and I am in good relations with my family. I feel my body, brain, and soul are getting healthy now.

With hope and confidence I am moving ahead. Nothing is impossible.

Puspa D.
(June 1991)

———————

Une Alcoolique à Paris

Paris, France

t a certain time of my life, I heard about AA through an American woman for whom I worked. She never spoke about my alcoholism but kept referring to a friend of hers who was a member of AA in California.

At that time I hadn't lost my husband, my children, my social position, and honestly thought I could stop "when I wanted." However, I drank more and more, although I kept trying not to do so, until 1970 when I attempted suicide. I didn't really want to die, but could just find no other way to deliver my children from their alcoholic mother. I really thought I was doing the best for them. My last gift!

But God had other projects for me, and I woke up in a hospital three days later.

It took me another three months to contact AA. During that time I didn't drink but felt miserable. Finally, I looked up Alcooliques Anonymes in the phone book, found the number and address at the American Church in Paris, and called. It was the first time I admitted that "alcoolique" was something concerning me.

I didn't find the courage to go that day but I called again the next day, and it took me five hours to go from my home to the church (normally a trip of about thirty minutes) because I was so afraid of what I was doing, committing myself with alcoholics who I thought were all bums. This was nearly twenty years ago when AA wasn't very well known in France, and women alcoholics were a complete disgrace.

Day by day, year by year, AA has progressed in France, and from 25 groups at that time we are now 320. I feel very lucky to have been part of this growth.

I couldn't guess at that time what AA could bring into my life, but from the very beginning I had the possibility to see the program work in other people's lives. I understood the hard way that if I wanted what they had, I would have to follow the Steps and get involved. AA has given me the opportunity to be an active part in my own life and stop putting the blame on others.

AA has "come of age" in France, and so have I. May God help me to keep close to AA if I want to keep on living my life in sobriety as a wonderful adventure.

Annie C. B.
(July 1970)

MY NAME IS ADOLFO

Caracas, Venezuela

My name is Adolfo, and I am an alcoholic. Now, thanks to God, to the program of Alcoholics Anonymous, and to every AA group that shares its experiences, strength, and hope with me, I find myself in a process of recovery.

Even though it was difficult enough for me to recognize the illness, it was even more difficult to admit that I was seized with it. But practically never did I drink without getting drunk; never did I stop suffering from the aftereffects of drunkenness (hangover), which almost always brought moral depressions, remorse, guilty feelings, insecurity, unjustified fears, nervous tension, senseless anguish, states of despair.

I started to drink while I was in the United States Air Force. Two years later, I was receiving an "undesirable" discharge in the middle of the Korean War, everything due to the failures provoked by alcoholism. Later, in civilian life, I tried to finish my education, starting my third year in the university. But there was a mental barrier that impeded me. I did not know what to do with my life. There was no reason for existing, no goal to pursue, and therefore I lost all aspiration and, at the same time, all control of myself, for I dedicated myself to drinking.

The last four years that I was in the United States, I worked in a steel mill, and I do not remember ever working a complete week. I used to work only enough to recover physically and economically, in order to continue the endless spree. Those workdays were like small rests that I made in the long race of my alcoholism.

When I reached the limit of my confusion and found myself with no course in life, no confidence in anybody, and no faith in anything, I wanted to escape from myself. I wandered through Mexico and Central America, getting drunk with every kind of liquor that appeared. At the end of eight months, I returned to my native country, Nicaragua, accompanied of course by alcohol, which got me into a mess that kept me in jail for forty-seven days. The press and radio took my name, threw it down to the floor, and kicked it around, which caused a deep psychological impact. It still amazes me that I did not land in an insane asylum.

How many times and in how many places did I get thrown in jail for drunkenness? In El Salvador, in Costa Rica, in Nicaragua, once in Las Vegas, Nevada, several times in New Mexico, and again in California. If I wasn't jailed for being drunk in more countries, it was because I didn't remain long enough. And yet it took a lot of effort to accept my alcoholic condition, even though I had converted myself into a man who drank day, night, and dawn without taking care of home, family, job, or responsibilities. I only took care of the god Bacchus. I used to transport myself to his temple, which is transporting oneself to another world, a world of the unreal, a strange world where anything can pass as normal, a world where I used to submerge myself until almost drowning.

Nevertheless, with the help of God, manifested through several brothers who for some time were besieging me, I came to Alcoholics Anonymous. I was in a really deplorable state, without money, job, home, faith, and perhaps even hope.

Today, I have reached one year of not tasting even a single sip of alcohol. Although I have not recovered everything, I have at least the essentials for I have a job and I have my wife and children with me. It was a Fourth of July that I suffered from my last drunkenness, an afternoon when, along with other bar brothers, I went to the cemetery to bury an unknown person. We were attracted by the mere fact that they were offering liquor there. My mother, as so many other times, found out where I was and waited for me at the gate of the cemetery to take me home.

The following day, I visited the Colon Group in Managua, Nicaragua, where my true recovery started, later going on to follow up the treatment in the Caracas, Venezuela groups (Los Chorros, San Roman, and Los Salesianos). And at that time, I made comparisons with the independence celebrations of the United States (July 4) and of Venezuela (July 5). I felt as though I had liberated myself from the fictitious and dismal world of alcohol. I still feel no need for the crutches of booze. For me, July 4 and 5 constitute the date of my own independence.

This first year of sobriety in Alcoholics Anonymous has been difficult. There have been obstacles; there have been problems. What made my stay in AA more difficult was that I could not conceive of a Superior Being, because of the simple reason that I already had my own superior being — alcohol. Since I was never a religious person, I arrived at AA without knowing how to pray, without knowing any prayer.

But I had the desire to remain in the Fellowship. With more effort and sincerity, an incipient conception of a Superior Power was being forged, which I still preserve. It is rudimentary, but I keep cultivating it with the hope of some day seeing the flourishing of some ineffable fruits.

Thus, until today at least, I am getting further away from that first drink, which is the one that inevitably leads me to complete disaster, and from whence I came scarcely 365 twenty-four hours ago.

Adolfo B.
(May 1971)

MY NAME IS CARL

Stockholm, Sweden

I am a Finn who has lived in Sweden for the last ten years. I am also a recovered alcoholic who nowadays enjoys every minute of this happy and wonderful life under the ever-shining sun of sobriety. And I am grateful to the God I came to know through AA for this serenity and peace of mind.

I began my intake of alcohol in my very early youth. Between my early teens and twenties, I was a periodic drinker. I drank mainly to get up the courage to fetch a girl for a weekend dance. I was too shy to do it sober.

In my teens, I noticed I had no manners when drinking. I became aggressive and often had fistfights with my neighbors. Once, I hit a German soldier and was shot in the back by his comrades. When I woke up, I was in the hospital. My legs were paralyzed. The doctor said to me, "It's a wonder you're still alive!"

I decided never to take a drink again. All I wanted was to get up and walk. When I left the hospital, I was not completely recovered (I never will be), but I was able to walk, slowly. I soon forgot my promise to stay sober, and things started to get worse. From seventeen to twenty-one, my spells of dryness became a little longer, because of army service in World War II. First, we fought Russians and then Germans. When peace came, we had to pay a high price for our independence. Our country was poverty-stricken; the war had brought much misery.

At that time, I lived only for drinking and drank only to live. I no longer had control over alcohol. Saturday night ran into Sunday and very soon ran on through the week. I became an entirely different person, off in my own little world. I was totally unable to drink normally. I had such a compulsion to drink that there were not many sober hours. I was sick and shaky in the mornings, afraid of meeting people, scared of noisy traffic. I had to take that first drink every morning, and it set up the reaction which commanded me to drink until I passed into coma.

At twenty-one, I had been taken into custody over a hundred times for drunkenness in public places. The recovery hours, in a cold police cell without any medical aid, were torture that often brought me close to insanity, and when they kicked me out, my only consolation was a bottle. Sometimes I was back in that cold cell after only a few hours.

At last, I was sent to prison because of my violent habits when drinking. But not even in prison was I sober all the time. A drink of some sort could be obtained, but there was punishment if I was caught. I spent many weeks in an isolated cell on bread and water — no smoking, no reading, and no bedclothes. But this punishment never stopped me.

When I came out of prison, I was able to keep my sobriety for two months with the help of AA. Then I married a young girl, a fellow student, and on our wedding day I began to drink with the guests. A week later, I again tried my wings on the AA program.

I bought some property in Helsinki and began building a house. For a year and a half, I had only a few slips. I thought I was succeeding quite well and got an inspiration to start a new large building for shops. You can guess how it all ended!

Now I realize my dreams were flying too high, and my drinking flew as high as my dreams. I made life miserable for my wife, for my friends who had helped me before, and for myself. Our marriage lasted four years and ended in divorce. I was alone again in the world. Thank God, we had no children.

After a year or so, I married another girl, very pretty and charming. As part of adjusting myself to living a married life again, I decided not to drink anymore, even though she liked to drink now and then. I founded a large business, and in the beginning it succeeded. But a brandy shop was situated nearby. Early in the morning, I would count the seconds until that brandy shop opened, so I could get bottles of beer and brandy for the day. Things went on like this. I found that I couldn't put on the brakes. It all ended in complete bankruptcy, mental and financial.

Fear and self-pity moved in with me. I was bitter and resentful. My violent drinking habits scared my pregnant wife. She called for the police, instead of AA, and I was locked up in a cell again for a long, long time. I had no place in a free society, because my wife, friends, and others had been constantly in fear of me. Now my mind was as gloomy as the gray walls of my cell.

After release, I fled from my native country to some of the faraway places of the world, but the burning desire for alcohol followed me everywhere. Some ten years ago, police escorted me from Aden to Sweden. I had done something dreadful in my blackout drinking. My hands were bloody. (Please do not close me from your friendship. I need all of you in AA, for I still have a long way to go on our program.)

As I write this, I no longer have my second wife. I have not seen her and my son for ten years. I still love her, but I don't even know where she and my son are living now. I know only that her new husband is an old AA friend of mine and that they have more children. I hope they are happy.

To me now, my awful past is only a great warning mark on the road of this happy sobriety I have today. Looking back, I wonder how I could have lived such a hard and stupid life, on the verge of insanity, especially when I had within reach this new way of life, which is so wonderful.

Often, very often, I ask myself for what reason I began to drink excessively. I couldn't have inherited this illness, as I came from a non-drinking family. My four brothers never had troubles with alcohol. One is a sea captain; one is a rancher; one is a clerk for the city consul; one is a prosperous farmer. I was supposed to be the most intelligent of us all, but my brothers succeeded in their careers, and I didn't. Sometimes I think it was that bullet in my back that caused conflicts in my brain, but I have to admit I had an addiction to alcohol even before I was shot. In success I drank; in failure I drank.

During my first year of AA I learned a lot, but I don't think I started to live AA or to apply much of what I learned. I was bypassing many of the Twelve Steps and was not keen on studying any of them thoroughly. Then, about ten years ago, I knew I couldn't afford to bypass them anymore. I realized I was being given my very last chance for recovery. I devoted myself entirely to the AA program. I began to trust more in the God I had come to know through AA. Except for bad memories which surface now and then, an almost complete serenity occupies my mind.

Thanks to God, I'll soon have ten candles burning on my AA birthday cake. For ten years I have really lived. I didn't live before.

C. J. G.
(June 1970)

SOMETHING REVOLUTIONARY

Nairobi, Kenya

I had my first blackout at the age of six. I was born into a family of alcoholics — an alcoholic father, an alcoholic mother, and alcoholic uncles — and my childhood memories are full of images of alcohol. My parents drank daily and neglected us children. Their quarrels ensured that we didn't have the peace, parental love, and nurturing needed for our growth.

One day, as my father and his friends were enjoying their favorite drink, made from honey and herbs, I went to sit with them. I remember him occasionally passing his glass to me for a sip. The sips eventually turned into gulps. I cannot recall what happened afterward. All I can remember is waking up the following morning with a feeling of nausea. My head and my stomach were aching. Later I realized that I'd suffered from a blackout followed by a hangover, one of many in the years to come. I was six years old.

One year later, my parents could not stand each other's drinking, and so they parted. This was the beginning of a most traumatic period in my life. With Mother gone and a drunk for a father, I and my brother were left on our own. Nobody showed us what was good and what was bad. Food became scarce, and we were reduced to scavenging the neighborhood for survival.

My father married again. Living with a stepmother was a nightmare. Both my father and my stepmother turned me and my brother into objects to be abused and ridiculed. This made me start hating the world. Life continued like that until 1955, when Mother decided to take custody of us.

This was at the height of the independence struggle in Kenya. The Mau Mau war of independence was raging. For a single mother, life was simply impossible. Mother decided to start distilling and selling an illicit alcohol called *chang'aa* ("kill me quick") or *machozi ya simba* ("lion's tears"), so called by those who drank the stuff. It is a very potent African gin. The profits she made enabled her to send us to school.

Soon I was an expert at distilling the stuff. Usually, I took over from my mother when she passed out. My life now oscillated between school, and selling and drinking *chang'aa*. This went on throughout my teenage years.

At the age of twenty, I was apprenticed to an advertising agency in Nairobi where I began to learn graphic design. This is the period when my drinking escalated. The advertising agency was sponsoring me for evening classes in design. Instead of attending classes, however, I used the opportunity to drink. Mostly I drank myself to oblivion. The agency soon discovered my tricks and fired me. But I landed another job almost immediately. It is important to mention that in the area of design at that time in Kenya, expatriates dominated. This helped bloat my ego. I thought I was great by being associated with them, and as a way of showing off, I drank from bar to bar, buying people drinks, and announcing to all and sundry my unique skills and opportunities.

However, it did not take long for my new employers to learn that I had a problem with drinking, and they found it necessary to do away with me. I was without a job once again. But as luck would have it, I was soon again employed in another advertising agency — and soon fired, once my new employers realized the kind of young man I was.

Now I had built such a reputation for myself that no agency in town wanted to touch me. In the streets and without a job, my life was miserable. Fear and self-pity started to grip me. The bottle, which I loved dearly, became my only consolation. The more I stayed out of a job, the more I sank into the mire of alcoholism. I spent days and nights at the drinking dens to forget my woes.

One evening after a rather long spree, two policemen stopped me. They wanted to know why I had become a nuisance after drinking. My reply was that they had no business interfering with other people's right to drink and be merry. They attempted to arrest me. In my stupor, I put up a fight. Of course they overpowered me, and had me charged the following day with being drunk and disorderly. I was in jail for two months.

When I came out of jail, I got a job in a printing concern. My ego convinced me that working for a printer was less prestigious than my advertising work. I was frustrated more often and my drinking picked up. Several warning letters didn't do the trick. One morning in June 1975, I went to work with a hangover as usual. My boss mentioned that I was smelling like a brewery, something I deeply resented. With anger and resentment seething inside me, I continued with work. In the evening, I headed straight for a *chang'aa* den to soothe my nerves. I cannot remember much of the evening. All I can remember is trying to wake up and dress for work the following morning. But what happened next shocked me. I fell out of the bed and immediately there was blood and water everywhere. People ran toward me and forced me back on the bed. I struggled but was overpowered. I was in a hospital and had been put on IV drips. I learned later that I'd been in a coma for three months. I'd fallen headfirst from the first story of the flat I shared, injuring my head and brain.

The next time I awoke, I found I'd been tied to the bed. Immediately, I was seized by a king-sized craving for a drink. Several family members visited me that day and were delighted that I was awake. But they stared at me with surprise and consternation when I requested that they bring me fruit juice laced with alcohol. Later I learned that none of them thought I would live. Indeed some had concluded I was dying, and were coming to see me for the last time. Eventually, however, I was discharged, and I limped out of the hospital on a pair of crutches. I was unable to see clearly, so an eye patch was put on one of my eyes.

When I got to the flat where I lived, I found out that my employers had written me a letter terminating my services, claiming that I had overstayed my sick leave. I was forced to leave my flat, and I went to stay with my mother. When I arrived at her house, I found a totally different mother from the one I had known. She was happy and joyous. She was clean and her face radiated with confidence and satisfaction. I was taken aback. This was not the mother I was used to. Something revolutionary had happened to her. Yes, she was sober.

She talked about a Fellowship called Alcoholics Anonymous; she said that was what had changed her. She talked of a certain priest who had come from the United States and helped her sober up in the first Swahili-speaking AA group in Kenya. She was recommended to him as someone with an alcohol problem — her drinking was well-known within the community.

The priest and my mother tried to bring me to AA, but I wouldn't hear of it. In fact, I resented that priest. I thought he had converted my mother. I had never heard of AA before, so my denial took the form of suspicion.

I continued to drink. The fact that I was walking on crutches was not a hindrance. By this time, however, a feeling of hopelessness had overwhelmed me. Fear, self-pity, and resentments were the order of my existence. Now I began to drink in order to die. Many were the times that I was carried home, dead drunk, by a sister of mine whom I loved very much. Unfortunately, she later became alcoholic and died of alcohol-related causes in her early thirties. I was also to lose a brother, also in his early thirties, because of alcoholism.

One evening as I was coming from a visit to the hospital, accompanied by my sister, the urge to drink took hold of me. We were just a few yards away from home. I gave my sister my medicines to carry home and headed for one of my favorite drinking dens. Inside, I found many of the men sitting there in different stages of withdrawal. This affected me. They were waiting for the stuff to be brought in from wherever it came from. Then my sister walked in. She reminded me that I'd promised our mother I would that evening attend an AA meeting.

In spite of myself, I obliged. But like any other alcoholic, my intention was not attend the meeting so as to sober up; I only agreed to go to prove to my mother that things like AA were not for me. Immediately after the meeting, I reasoned, I could go out and drink. That would make my mother and her priest friend stop bothering me. I was then twenty-seven years old.

I'm grateful that I attended that meeting. I found people whom I knew, and they were no longer the withdrawn, suffering alcoholics I had known. Instead, their faces shone with a brightness that reflected an inner peace. They shared their experience, strength, and hope. I was surprised at what I heard. Their stories sounded familiar. I was particularly impressed by the sharing of one member whom I'd known before. He told of one incident when he had left us drinking *chang'aa* in one den only to come back moments afterward, bleeding, one of his ears having been chopped off. He vividly described how we had applied first aid on his ear using *chang'aa* which we had been made to believe acted as a medicine for all human ills.

If such a fellow had sobered up, I thought, I also could.

When I was asked to introduce myself, I did so, for the first time referring to myself as an alcoholic. At this moment, I felt as if a heavy load had been removed from my back. I was left with a feeling of self-assurance and hope. From that day on, I have kept going to AA meetings. That was twenty-two years ago.

I can say that it has continued to get better, one day at a time. AA has replaced hopelessness with hope. Today I live in the knowledge that whatever happens, God is always by my side. I have learned to accept my status as an alcoholic who is recovering.

Many things have happened in the last twenty-two years. Of much importance is the fact that I've managed to advance my education. I graduated two years ago with an advanced diploma in counseling. This has enabled me to help fellow alcoholics reach sobriety. I married when I had over three years' sobriety in AA and now have four children, aged eighteen years to nine years. My mother died with fifteen years of sobriety in AA. She passed on to me the AA message, which I am also passing on to other suffering alcoholics. Recently, I was elected the chairperson of the Nairobi intergroup. I hope to give the best of myself in this service to help AA reach out to many in Kenya.

The final message I would like to give is this: AA may or may not get me to heaven, but it surely got me out of hell.

Michael S.
(April 1998)

Trinidad

Trinidad, West Indies

I was born on a small sugar estate in southern Trinidad, and I am the only child of my parents. I was loved by them and by many of the people on the estate, due to my sincerity and obedience. I was very bright in school, but I was already having casual drinks now and again with my parents. Then came the time I took a couple of drinks before leaving for school in the morning, and this went on.

I had to leave school when I was sixteen and go to work, but I wanted to take shorthand, typing, and bookkeeping. I knew my parents could afford to send me to commercial school, but they denied this to me. That Christmas, I got drunk on wine with some friends, and on Boxing Day morning, I had the remorse feeling. I was so sick, I went into a pond to have a bath, but I had to have two drinks of rum before I went in, for the coldness. After the bath, I started all over drinking again.

One year after I started working, I got married. Shortly after, I had to leave the job in the sugar factory — I was assistant electrician — and go to San Fernando town and begin working as a cinema operator for seven dollars a week. I had to leave several good jobs like that because of my drinking.

After two years of marriage, my wife had a baby girl, and two years after the birth of the baby, my wife divorced me, and I never saw that baby again and the baby never saw me, not until she was thirty-two years of age and had two children of her own. (She had by then become a qualified nurse in Canada. Her mother told her that I had died, but some of her other relatives told her I was alive, and so she decided to come see me. She came to Trinidad one carnival week, and she met me, and then we became known to each other as two new friends who had been apart for quite some time. This was after I was sober.)

I have ten other children and a second wife; they, too, suffered from my alcoholism for some years, until AA came into my life. As soon as I found AA, there was great change in my life and in my family life also. I came to AA without one cent in my possession, not even

81

a cent to put in the hat when it was passed at meetings. At times, there was nothing in my home to eat, and my children had not been able to get a proper education.

AA has enabled me to help my children during my sober years, to give them some education. Love and affection are among our family once more. From my beginning in the program, I have been very active, for thirteen years now. And I have decided to stay on until I have departed from this life. Thanks to the founders of AA and the many friends who have labored to bring AA to where it is today, I and my family are living very happily. And I always try to carry the message to alcoholics everywhere.

Thanks to God, I found AA, and my life has become manageable once more. I can recommend it to anyone who has a drinking problem; it helped me, so it can help anyone.

J. S.
(April 1980)

PEACE AT LAST

Rizal, Philippines

The sun had just risen, and a mist was coming off the Neckar River as it flowed slowly past the outskirts of the town of Heidelberg in West Germany. An elderly man stood by the river's edge, fishing. It was a tranquil scene, but as I stood there, I felt anything but tranquil. I had pulled my car over to the side of the road and gotten out, coming back from another night of nonstop drinking, as I had been doing for months on end. I felt full of chaos and confusion, and, having come rather unexpectedly upon the sight of such deep peace, I began to experience a profound sense of sadness. I knew that serenity was not for me.

My life revolved around alcohol — and with it, pain and sadness. Intuitively, I knew I was not only killing myself but destroying all the good in my life. I returned to the car and drove off — to get a drink; and I continued to drink for the next thirteen years. By the time I finally hit bottom and sought help, sadness, turmoil, and a sense of despair had become a way of life.

Like most alcoholics, I used all the usual "reasons" for not stopping drinking: "I won't be able to sleep at night"; "My life will be too boring if I quit drinking"; "If I stop, people will think I have a problem" (no need to worry; they already knew). But I had one real reason that kept me from stopping: I knew that if I did quit drinking, I would almost certainly have to begin looking into myself, and I was very much afraid of what I would find. I had little enough peace while drinking, but I feared I'd lose even that if I ever stopped.

Yet, like most alcoholic fears, this one proved false. A few weeks after I stopped drinking, I was attending a seminar on alcoholism at a rehabilitation place in New Hampshire. I was learning that I had a disease and that I could do something about it. A great weight seemed to be lifting off my shoulders — and out of my life. Between the talks, I often took long walks in the woods. It was December, and snow had already fallen. One afternoon as I was walking in the woods, it suddenly came to me that I was more at peace with myself than I could recall ever having been. A first touch of serenity had come to me. I experienced an overwhelming feeling of thankfulness to God for lifting me from the alcoholic sadness that bordered on despair.

In the seven years since I've been sober, the feeling of peace in my life has continued to grow slowly. I now find that when I come upon a scene of real beauty and serenity — a tropical sunset, a clear autumn day in New England, snow in the Rockies — my mind may return to that early morning in Heidelberg, and I once again thank God and the Fellowship of Alcoholics Anonymous for having brought me out of the chaos and despair of alcoholic drinking to the new and infinitely better life that I can now enjoy.

D. M.
(February 1981)

Part Three

Growth

'More at Home in This World'

Vilnius, Lithuania

My name is Romas. I am a resident of the city of Vilnius, in Lithuania. Alcohol burst into my life when I was in my teens, but the first real problems cropped up when I was twenty-four. At that time I was a student, and I realized one day that my thirst for knowledge was being smothered by some other kind of thirst. Still I believed in myself, and the future seemed bright. After graduation I married and it seemed to me for some time that alcohol problems had sunk into the past along with my bachelorhood. They had not! In a short while I once again became an ardent bar-goer (if this is the right word). My inclination for alcohol was ever growing and, as the years passed by, it robbed me of my health and time. My every effort to break away proved to be a failure. Short intervals of sobriety would give me some hope, but life in general was a torture to me and my family.

All this went on for over ten years. Little by little I drew into my shell, the feelings of depression and lack of self-confidence were constantly deepening. I was being trampled by mental and physical inconvenience, and life seemed impossible. More and more often I would catch myself sadly reflecting on killing myself. I was lonesome, torn away from myself and others.

A year or so ago I changed my job, and new surroundings helped me pull myself together. Last winter I consulted a doctor and decided to try once again to stop drinking. A good expert in psychology managed to revive in me spiritual forces, and it was he who advised me to contact AA.

I wrote a letter to America and soon got an answer from Washington, D.C. together with a couple of booklets about the program and activities of AA. Besides, a friend of mine had the "Great Book" translated into Lithuanian. I read the book and it made me feel more at home in this world. A group of AA members from the United States visited Vilnius in summer this year. With two friends of mine I invited them to my place. We had a superb time. These AA members strengthened our spirits. And so, the first group of AA was born in Lithuania. It consisted of three people. Together with our guests we also took part in a meeting in one of the medical care centers where a number of physicians were present along with alcoholics in treatment. We decided to have an AA meeting. The constituent assembly took place on July 3. It was the beginning.

The AA group now consists of fifteen people, including four women. We meet once a week. We have lots of problems because we are as yet green in sobriety. Together we read the "Great Book," discuss our program, and share experiences.

We were glad to meet a Canadian woman of Lithuanian descent, Helen, who is in AA for ten years. She enriched us with her experience.

The book *Twelve Steps and Twelve Traditions* is now being translated into Lithuanian, and we are looking forward to meeting more and more AA members from around the world.

Lithuanian AA is making its first steps. We are trying to broaden our ties with other people. We plan to publish an article in the Lithuanian press about AA and its goals. We think of setting up a coordinating center to "advertise" AA and establish contacts with other groups. We are in the process of negotiating with the authorities about permanent quarters for AA.

Our group is sure to grow, and I hope every alcoholic will find his way to God and to victory. Perestroika and democratization which are on the way in our country have triggered the rebirth of the Lithuanian nation, and this revival of spirit is impossible for me without sobriety.

I have a dream that the noble activities of AA will not only reach into the hearts of those who suffer but will also win the approval of society at large.

Let me express heartiest thanks to our "godfathers" — three beautiful AA members: Charlie, Ted, and Bill. They "baptized" us in Vilnius this summer.

Romas O.
(June 1989)

BACK TO THE FUTURE

Kyushu, Japan

t is nothing short of miraculous that Alcoholics Anonymous exists in some 150 countries today. But the on-the-ground reality in most nations is that the success achieved by AA in its native United States remains far from being fully duplicated.

Take Japan, for example, where AA is just now starting to really take off. I'm a member of both Japanese-speaking and English-speaking home groups in Kyushu, the westernmost of Japan's four main islands. I'm extremely grateful AA is here. Without our Fellowship, I wouldn't be sober today. Yet plenty of basic message-carrying legwork still needs to be done in Japan.

The Japanese-language version of the Big Book was first published in 1979, forty years after the English version. In several respects, the general state of AA in Japan today resembles that of American AA at mid-century. As of 1998, according to the Kyushu-Okinawa Central Office, there were about 250 AA groups in Japan and roughly 4,000 AA members nationwide. Note that Japan is a nation of 125 million people where alcoholism is no small problem.

There is no regular AA meeting in the city of 250,000 people where I live, so frequent meeting attendance requires some travel. Maintaining anonymity is not difficult, as the terms "Alcoholics Anonymous" and "Twelve Steps" are totally unknown to the general public. Indeed, relatively few physicians in this part of western Japan (including doctors directly involved with inpatient alcoholism treatment!) have ever heard of AA, much less Doctor Silkworth's disease concept of alcoholism.

AA birthday chips, bumper stickers, and sobriety calendars are hand-carried back into Japan by members traveling abroad, as such "recovery goods" are not available here. Japanese members do not listen to speaker tapes: there are none. The AA Grapevine is not translated into Japanese, but the national Japan Service Office and regional central offices put out their own publications. There are now Japanese translations of most Conference-approved literature, but we're still looking forward to *As Bill Sees It*. The important work of carrying the AA message into prisons has recently been initiated.

Japanese AA members are typically older, overwhelmingly male, and have experienced lower drinking bottoms than many of their counterparts in other places. These demographics are highly reminiscent of AA in the United States years ago, and reflect the social stigma and misunderstanding still strongly associated with alcoholism. Despite all these differences in developmental stages, however, AA in Japan is essentially the same as AA anywhere else.

We open our Japanese meetings in the usual way, by reciting the AA Preamble. We then read part of chapter three from the Big Book, followed by the standard portion of chapter five beginning "Rarely have we seen a person fail . . . " A few weeks back, I was asked to read the Twelve Steps in English at the appropriate time. Sometimes we read the Ninth Step Promises too. There are coffee and snacks, and we are self-supporting.

Meeting topics often come from the Japanese version of *Daily Reflections*. After swapping experience, strength, and hope for ninety minutes, we close with the Serenity Prayer (from our seats, without holding hands). We were cleaning up after one recent meeting when a middle-aged woman rode up on a bicycle to inquire about help for her father, an active alcoholic. She knew next to nothing about AA (there's no contact number in the local phone book), but had heard through word-of-mouth about our small band of nondrinking drunks.

Such encounters are currently infusing Japanese AA with a contagious enthusiasm and pioneer-like determination. There is a growing awareness that we are involved in a great nascent enterprise. As our worldwide Fellowship enters the new millennium, Alcoholics Anonymous is starting to enter the mainstream of Japanese society.

Across Japan today, new groups are forming and new meetings are starting up. Here in Kyushu, the first-ever AA group in Oita Prefecture (the equivalent of an American state) was founded in 1998. More and more people (not all of them alcoholics) are being exposed to AA at open roundups and similar events. Younger and younger Japanese (not all of them men) are joining AA. Thanks to the ongoing efforts of Japan's "good old-timers," future growth will be handled by a service structure now solidly in place.

I receive the *Loners-Internationalists Meeting (LIM)* newsletter, a bimonthly English "meeting in print" for AAs scattered throughout the world, and I've learned to appreciate that, compared to AA's state of development in many nations, AA in Japan is quite progressive and advanced.

None of the above observations are intended to be critical of AA in Japan or anywhere else. Rather, in pondering AA's future course, such local snapshots may help remind us that the global reality of Alcoholics Anonymous is not monolithic. The English-speaking countries where AA enjoys a vast membership and wide public acceptance represent wonderful exceptions. This degree of success is not yet the norm.

The past sixty years have demonstrated that Alcoholics Anonymous can take root and flourish anywhere, among anyone. At the same time, the bigger picture suggests that we cannot take AA's next century for granted. In my tiny corner of the AA universe, like in countless other tiny corners, the future of AA lies in traveling "back into the past."

But we're getting there. Together, one day at a time.

Bill U.
(January 2000)

ALCOLISTI ANONIMI IN ITALIA

La Canada, California

The thirty or so "GSRs" meeting in an AA meeting room this April Saturday morning were reporting on the activities, progress, and problems of their home groups. Myriad topics were covered but certain themes kept reemerging — more financial support for the Central Office and what to do about the young people coming to our meetings whose primary addiction is narcotics.

I felt like I'd never left home. But I was 7,000 miles from home and the placards adorning the walls were strange to these American eyes. After all, "I Dodici Passi di AA" and "Le Dodici Tradizioni di AA" aren't part of the decor in my meeting rooms. And I am unaccustomed to thinking of God as "Signore," as in "Signore concedimi la Serenita di accetare le cose che non posso cambiare. . . ." I was in the meeting room of the Nuova Vita (New Life) Italian AA group in the heart of Rome at a regular district meeting of AA groups from four Italian provinces, from Naples to north of Rome and east to the Adriatic. But the familiar subjects of the discussions made me feel quite at home, as Sara A., a thirty-five-year American resident of Rome, summarized for me.

Many Americans traveling abroad attend the English-language AA meetings listed in the International AA Directory. I attended many in Rome, where there are eleven meetings a week at three different locations, meetings that attract people of all nationalities. But this time I thought it would also be interesting to look into the indigenous homegrown Italian AA, and with the encouragement of the Grapevine and the General Service Office I was put into contact with some key Italian AAs.

The history of Italian AA is not entirely indigenous or homegrown, however, and one must go back to those English-language groups for its genesis. The story goes that as early as 1947 an American journalist put an ad in the *Stars and Stripes* newspaper inviting other alcoholics to contact him. From that ad came the first English-language meeting in Rome, and by the early nineteen-sixties it had found a home at St. Paul's (Anglican) Church, only a few blocks from the central railway station. In 1987 there were five meetings a week there, plus an Al-Anon meeting. An Italian group also meets there on different days or at different times, and the ancient walls of the stone crypt where they gather offers space for the familiar AA placards, slogans, and notices in both languages.

Sometime in the early seventies, an Italian named Carlo C. started coming to those meetings, and an American woman named Mia translated or at least summarized for him. It's said it took him a year and a half to achieve sobriety, but with time he was joined by Giovanni, Ermano, and Yolanda, the latter being the first Italian woman to reach AA sobriety. These people formed the nucleus of the first all Italian group of Alcolisti Anonimi.

The same pattern evolved in Florence, where Sylvano came to the then-small English-language meeting being held in the crypt of St. James American Church. Here an English lady named Jocelyn translated for Sylvano, and he quickly became sober and attracted other Italians. Thus the first Italian group in Florence came into being, and today it shares the same meeting room with the English-language group.

At this point, an intriguing secondary story must be told. It concerns a book entitled *A Man Running Away,* written by Carlo Coccioli in the early seventies. This Carlo was not an alcoholic and although he was a Florentine, he was living in Mexico City and wrote in Spanish. And the book was fiction, a novel that dealt with an alcoholic and his experience with AA, providing readers with an accurate picture of the Fellowship and its principles. It was translated into Italian and became very popular in Italy.

An American resident of Florence recalls that one Sunday morning in the mid-seventies he had just been released from jail, again, and was at a bar "getting well" when he happened to read a review of that book in the Rome *Daily American.* He was almost broke, hungover, shaky and despondent, but the review touched something within him. Knowing there was an AA meeting in Rome, and not knowing there was at least one in Florence, he boarded an express train for Rome and attended his first meeting that night. Although he didn't get sober for a few months, he did start attending the Florence meeting and today is enjoying a mature sobriety.

The nonalcoholic author of this novel plays an even larger role in Italian AA, according to Jocelyn. Coccioli visited Florence, as he often did, in 1974, and along with Jocelyn and Malcolm of the English-language group planned and staged a series of four informational meetings about Alcoholics Anonymous. Carlo Coccioli was able to get notices in the Florence papers that said in effect, "Come see what we're about." The meetings were very well attended by doctors, clergy, social workers, interested laymen, and an occasional alcoholic, Sylvano among them.

Such are the mysterious ways of Alcoholics Anonymous that a work of fiction written in Spanish by an Italian nonalcoholic living in Mexico came to play a pivotal role in the early history of Italian AA. The book has apparently not been translated into English.

Through the late seventies AA grew slowly, and in 1981 had about thirty groups. But in 1978 Roberto C., the current national secretary and once a journalist in the United States, translated a thirty-page "synopsis" of the Big Book. Ten or twelve members raised $1,000 among them to have it published and that accelerated the growth considerably. In the meantime they were working with the General Service Office in New York on an official translation of the Big Book. When it was completed in 1980, Roberto presented the first copy to Lois W. at the International Convention in 1980.

AA World Services, Inc., in New York, advanced the Italians $25,000 to underwrite the printing of their Big Book, a sum that was quickly repaid. Most of the stories, after that of Dr. Bob, are home-grown Italian success stories.

With that new ingredient, Italian AA began to grow very rapidly. But, as I was told by a number of Italian members, the problems of money, power, and prestige came to Italy, as they seem to come at some stage of AA growth in most places. The details are not important here. Suffice it to say that the outcome was the development of a group of trusted servants who believed strongly in the importance of adhering to the Traditions as essential guidelines for a successful Alcoholics Anonymous. Such belief on the part of the current trustees derives not from the fact that the Traditions are "American" but because the leaders know the history of AA here, are familiar with the struggles and conflicts that gave rise to the Traditions, and recognize their universality.

Growth continued and in 1987 there were an estimated 250 to 300 groups, with possibly 900 meetings a week. New groups continue to be formed at a rate of up to thirty a year, with the Central Office providing starter kits of the wall posters and a copy of each appropriate piece of literature. The Central Office now has one full-time employee.

Most of the U.S./Canada Conference-approved literature has been translated into Italian, with *AA Comes of Age* nearing completion; a daily meditation book is in progress.

Growth is slower in southern Italy in the more rural and poorer areas where the stigma of alcoholism is still great. (I heard of one wife who would not sanction her husband attending AA and risk it being known he was an alcoholic because he was, after all, a "government official," in this case a postal worker.) And, of course, the rural population is sparser and meetings fewer and farther apart. On the island of Sardinia, for example, a core group of five AAs use the phone frequently to keep in touch with their outlying members. In the mountain areas of the province of Abruzzi several members make regular journeys to meet and encourage the AAs who are far removed from regular meetings.

As to what they do about the new and generally young people with drug addictions who come to their meetings: "We encourage them and sustain them as best we can and then help them form their own Narcotics Anonymous groups," as one group reported. In Rome two such NA groups are the result.

How do suffering alcoholics with a desire to stop drinking get to AA in the first place? The most frequent answer I got was that they are referred by their doctors. In Italy, hospitals rather than jails are where drunks now end up and it's there that doctors can use their influence.

Many also come from seeing the telephone book listing, which is accompanied by a three-quarter-inch ad across the bottom of page one of the Rome directory, giving the address and phone of the central office as well as of the sixteen AA groups in the Rome area. The Italians are proud to point out that as a courtesy they include the English-language group.

There is also an active public information program that encompasses radio and TV public service announcements, interviews, and newspaper stories. Right now, AA is very popular with the media, but the AA committees are sensitive to the possibility of moving too fast and slipping across the line into promotion.

Since 1985, Italy has had its own AA publication, a handsomely produced bimonthly magazine patterned after the Grapevine. It's titled *Insieme in AA* and now has a 2,300 circulation.

In early May 1987, the Third Annual Conference of Alcolisti Anonimi was held in the Adriatic seaside city of Rimini. The theme was "Giving Is Receiving," and the agenda included workshops with such topics as "Pride: a Negative Attitude," "A Return to Basic Principles," and "How to Carry Help to Small Groups." Observers from Malta and Switzerland were present to learn how the Italian service structure works.

At the Constitutional Convention in 1984, a leadership cadre of ten national trustees was decided upon. Currently only five have been elected. A major item of business at the Rimini conference was to elect the additional five trustees. But it was found that problems of communication and procedure had arisen and it was decided to delay the election until the October convention. This was taken as a sign of the increasing maturity of an organization that might just as easily have plunged ahead in violation of its own guidelines.

The entire Rimini conference was held, as Sara A. put it, "in an atmosphere of calm, serenity, love, and tolerance," qualities not always present during the Fellowship's more volatile days only a few years ago, she indicated.

Programs for reaching out are producing tangible results and a justifiable sense of pride and progress. For example, AA was invited to send a panel to meet with the medical faculty of the University of Rome. And the Italian Armed Services invited them to make a presentation to the Non-Commissioned Officers' School.

In early April, Carlo E., a national trustee, met with the Via Napoli English-language group, outlined the progress and problems of the Italian groups, and suggested that perhaps there were suitable areas for cooperation. For example, between ten and fifteen percent of the phone calls for help or information received at the Central Office are from English-speaking people and some help on the phones would be appropriate, as would visits to English-speaking people at hospitals. And it was suggested that it might be useful for someone to serve as informal liaison between the two groups. Sara A., my translator, was appointed to that role and as such she attended the Rimini conference as an observer. Seven members volunteered to serve on a committee to explore these and other areas of possible cooperation.

An announcement was made at the Rimini conference by Carlo E. that perhaps typifies the optimistic and upbeat aura surrounding AA in Italy. He said that his home group would the following week celebrate its sixth birthday, and five of its members would be celebrating their fifth AA birthdays.

In reflecting over the rocky years just past, Carlo E. observes that "it hasn't been easy," but "AA will continue to grow." Roberto C., who has two more years to serve as the national secretary, says he will devote them to meeting with groups and talking "Traditions, Traditions, Traditions." He also bestows generous praise on the General Service Office in New York and its staff for the considerable amount of information and moral support they offered during the recent restructuring.

He summarizes aptly, saying, "Alcoholics Anonymous in Italy is alive and well . . . and safe."

E. K.
(January 1988)

⸺ ◉ ⸺

AA AMONG THE PYRAMIDS

Cairo, Egypt

According to the medical director of a privately operated psychiatric hospital in Cairo, "two foreign gentlemen" began to hold AA meetings in 1972 for alcoholic in-patients at this hospital. How long this continued is not known, although members of the present Cairo Home Group still call on patients at this hospital when requested to do so.

The present group, formed in 1978, has operated in Cairo continuously since then. Two Americans working in Cairo began the group with two meetings a week held at a church in Maadi (a residential suburb some distance from the heart of Cairo). Some time later an open AA meeting was begun on a Saturday evening in a church behind the U.S. Embassy compound. By 1984, the need was felt for a closed midweek meeting downtown, and a study/discussion group was started, bringing the total (as of February 1987) to four meetings per week in Cairo.

My affiliation with Cairo AA began mid-year in 1982, when I began work under contract for a U.S. consulting firm. At that time the Cairo Home Group consisted of some fifteen members, mostly from the U.S. or Europe, with a scattering of Egyptians. The group proved to be my real oasis of serenity in a land so different from what I had been accustomed to in the States. Noise, traffic, and stressful working conditions would ordinarily have made the comfort of alcohol most necessary to me if it had not been for the support and fellowship of that group of people — it was like finding a ready-made family of folks who indeed cared.

Just as life began to seem livable in Cairo, my firm's manager ordered a move to Alexandria — four hours away. It meant the end of frequent AA meetings, as there was no AA in Alexandria.

Acting on a hunch that there would be others in Alexandria who wanted the AA program, I placed a notice in a local expatriate weekly newsletter, stating the AA Preamble and giving a telephone contact for anyone interested. Another drunk wanting to sober up was found, then a third. By the end of 1982, we were meeting biweekly at the YMCA in Alexandria and by mid-1983 we numbered five regulars.

But there were others who came, mainly merchant seamen and men from warships in port, or the occasional passenger off a freighter or ocean liner. We had placed notices in the Seaman's Club and contacted large naval vessels to inform others of our presence there. Also we had noted our presence in the International AA Directory.

However, as fate would have it, the group dissolved with concurrent terminations of work contracts by the more active members. I was transferred back to Cairo and by the autumn of 1983, the Alexandria group became inactive.

The Cairo Home Group remained strong, however, with the total number of active members varying from ten to as many as twenty-five. A small handful of Egyptians who spoke some English were attending, too, and efforts to make our presence known to others of all nationalities continued. One locally published monthly, *Cairo Today*, carried information on our meetings, and for a while spot ads were placed in the *Egyptian Mail*, a weekly English-language newspaper.

In the summer of 1984, I had to go to the United States for some surgery but I returned to Cairo for a few months in 1985. As is the case in Cairo, there is a large turnover of the expatriate population so the group was quite different, with the exception of a few of the local Egyptians still present as a nucleus. Again I went back to my native land for another year, to clear up personal affairs, then to return in the summer of 1986, remaining in Cairo to study Arabic.

By this time, the need was felt to translate *Alcoholics Anonymous* into Arabic, if we were to make any inroads into dealing with the Arab-speaking people who suffered from alcoholism. Through individual contributions by interested members of the Cairo Home Group and an additional contribution by the group as a whole, the book was translated into Arabic, typed, proofread, and submitted to the General Service Office in New York.

Interestingly enough, the alcohol problem in Egypt is not one of high visibility. Some Arab-speaking countries prohibit its use — others do not. Islamic teachings express sharp moral disapproval of drinking alcohol specifically, although this prohibition is not universally accepted within the Arab world; and there are Christians, Jews, and others living in these lands who do not follow Islamic customs.

Another factor to be noted is that alcoholic beverages are as a rule prohibitively expensive for all but the wealthier people. The more pressing problem, according to medical authorities here, lies in the addiction of people to hashish and other narcotic drugs. Presently we welcome those with problems of drugs other than alcohol only at Saturday night open meetings. However, a Narcotics Anonymous group could prove most useful here and elsewhere in the Middle East.

As luck would have it, AA seems to be reactivating in Alexandria, with two or three active members now living there. Plans are underway for regular meetings and for contacting the merchant ships and naval vessels as before.

Such is the situation here in Egypt today. We continue to welcome tourists passing through — we get some of our best AA sharing when they come to our meetings. And so we look forward to meeting you the next time you come to take a look at the Pyramids. We are in the International AA Directory, and if all else fails, the medical unit of the U.S. Embassy will advise you of our whereabouts. Until then . . .

L. V.
(January 1988)

———◦◉◦———

LITERATURE LEADS THE WAY

Rio de Janeiro, Brazil

Alcoholics Anonymous in Brazil was founded in 1947 — twelve years after Dr. Bob's last drink. However, it took more than twenty-three years to have our literature translated into Portuguese, the national language. As a consequence, many of the old-timers, with the exception of a few who were able to read English, never read a word of AA literature, not even the Twelve Steps.

Even after the first translations of AA material became available in Portuguese, only a few were interested. "You don't need that," many would say. "Look at me! I have been sober for the last twenty years. Keep coming as I did, and don't drink for the next twenty-four hours."

Nevertheless, when I joined AA in 1979 I went to the literature, even though opportunities to discuss and clarify it were basically nonexistent — there were no Step meetings or Traditions meetings, at least that I knew about. So I decided to start talking about the Steps and Traditions in my testimonies. Very frequently, though, one of the old-timers, talking after me, would make opposite recommendations.

Early in 1983 I heard about a special meeting for newcomers and thought it might be an ideal place to introduce new members to AA literature. In the same year, while visiting New York, I had the opportunity to visit the General Service Office, where I bought the pamphlet, in English, "Guide for Leading Beginners Meetings." Returning to the group, along with some others, I proposed that we start such a beginners meeting as was described in the pamphlet. But the group conscience was against the innovation if it would mean converting one of the regular meetings into a newcomers meeting. The group already had three meetings a day, seven days a week. Before long, however, the group felt the need to expand the permanent office space it rented to accommodate additional meetings, such as an English-speaking meeting, a women's meeting, and a gay meeting (the last two of which never got off the ground). So when space became available on the same floor, the group administrative committee (steering committee) recommended that we take it, and that we start a beginners meeting.

Presently, after almost three years, we are maintaining three beginners meetings a week and the reactions have been enthusiastic.

By group conscience definition, beginners are considered as such up to six months of continuous sobriety. It is suggested that they attend both beginners and regular meetings. Old-timers are invited to the meetings but are asked not to speak. The space that we have can accommodate up to twenty people, and this number is normally filled by newcomers.

The meeting itself has a duration of two hours. The first half hour is dedicated to the explanation of a relevant AA topic or some aspect of the program: AA structure, AA literature, sponsorship, the meaning of anonymity, the Third Tradition, etc. Then the leader of the meeting asks each newcomer how his or her last twenty-four hours were. Not much is said about the more remote past. Half an hour before the end of the meeting, the leader gives general information such as local AA events, the financial situation of the group, and new literature that is available. The collection is taken, and the total of the collection is announced then and there to the group.

One of the by-products of this beginners meeting is the participation of these newcomers in the regular meetings, giving testimonies adorned with references to the Steps and Traditions so fluently that many old-timers have started thinking about reading the books. Curiosity about the "Twelve and Twelve" has prompted the group to adopt two meetings a week devoted to AA literature, including the Twelve Concepts for World Service, to replace two of the "old style" regular meetings.

Old-timers who were always claiming the group was breaking Traditions when we first started the beginners meetings now demand that two weekly meetings of open discussion be held (it must be said that we lovingly consider these meetings to be beginners meetings for old-timers).

Other groups in different parts of the country have become very much interested in our beginners meetings, and we have been asked to help implement similar meetings. The pamphlet "Guide for Leading Beginners Meetings" has been translated into Portuguese and has been distributed to all groups through our local AA magazine.

In August of 1987, AA in Brazil will be celebrating its 40th anniversary. For sure I will be crying and thanking God for having allowed me not to be drunk and alone, but surrounded by a chorale of 15,000 voices singing the Serenity Prayer.

Guaracy M.
(January 1988)

———◈———

ON A MAORI MARAE

Rotorua, New Zealand

As is the case with many countries throughout the world, New Zealand has a large indigenous population with a relatively high incidence of alcoholism. The number of Maori people seeking help has been on the increase in the last couple of years, and I believe this to be a direct result of AA carrying its message into prisons, institutions, hospitals, and schools. The AA Fellowship in New Zealand has also become conscious of the need to reach out to this section of the community in a more personal way, and in June 1987, the Central Area held its area assembly at Hawera, on a Maori Marae — the sacred meeting house and the heart of Maori culture and life. In July the Northern Area also held its assembly on a Maori Marae, at Kaitaia, in the far north, and I have high hopes that these meetings will be the forerunners of similar meetings throughout New Zealand. The planting of our seeds of hope and recovery are sometimes dependent on the site of their planting, and I believe the Maori Marae to be a very fertile place. It augurs well for the future.

My personal experiences with the Maori people have been limited to speaking at schools, Maori women's seminars, health programs, and our basic Twelfth Step calls. We have AA literature that has been translated into Maori and most of the Pacific Island languages — a mammoth task undertaken by a member of the Fellowship. Very little has been done through professional agencies to attract the Maoris, and of those who do come to AA, most are referred through court programs, assessment centers, or treatment facilities.

I have found through personal observation that those who remain within the Fellowship are usually the ones who have been twelfth-stepped by, or have had personal contact with, an AA member. Once sober, not all remain active within the Fellowship, though many may continue to maintain their sobriety and their peace of mind. The Maori culture is steeped in spiritual lore and spiritual beliefs, and their grasp of the spirituality of the program is almost instinctive. They are also a deeply religious people and find the practice of the principles of AA to be totally complementary to their religious beliefs.

Many Maori AA members are now becoming more involved in our Third Legacy — Service. There are many who have been active at the group level, serving their terms and rotating through the group service jobs, yet very few became involved in the overall service structure. Fortunately, this trend seems to be changing and Maoris are now involved in all areas of service, and in past years have been Conference delegates, area delegates, intergroup representatives, and, in 1986, delegate to the World Service Meeting. Also this year, a Maori member has been elected as chairperson of an area assembly.

Although there are no national figures available, I attended a local meeting recently, and of the twenty-three members present, eight were Maori; five of them attend meetings on a regular basis, have home groups, and participate in the group conscience.

Overall, AA in New Zealand seems to be going through exciting times. I am really excited by the number of young people coming into the program, and though most of them are dually addicted, they seem to have no problem leaving other addictions outside the doors of AA and bringing only their alcoholism into the meetings. We are perhaps fortunate that we have a Maori member with eight years of continuous sobriety who was also dually addicted and who, by his example of working the program for his alcoholism, has shown that his other addiction has been arrested also.

There is also a new breed of delegate within the service structure — younger, questioning, enthusiastic, and dedicated young people who are prepared to stand up and be counted and who are accepting their responsibilities with eagerness and a refreshing thirst for knowledge. Having been personally involved in the service structure for many years, I feel a warm sense of freedom that my time is passing and that for others the time is now. It will be an exciting time for our Fellowship in New Zealand.

Elsie T.
(January 1988)

By Conflict We Grew

Warsaw, Poland

My name is Wiktor and I'm an alcoholic. I am from Poland, though I've lived for the last two and one half years in the United States, where I hit my bottom in April 1983. At that time I was introduced very generally to the concept of AA, and I went to a few meetings. I was so happy with myself for staying sober, and I would go to the meetings from time to time just to hear the people talk about how horrible it was when they were drinking, and it would keep me remembering that I shouldn't drink myself.

After six months of being in this state of happiness from not drinking and making an occasional meeting, I finished writing a book — my profession is writing. In the past after finishing a book, I would go on a binge to celebrate and unwind. But this time, instead of going to the bar, I took a bus to Pennsylvania and checked myself into an alcoholic rehab facility. And I remember thinking that of course I didn't really need it (since I hadn't had a drink in six months), but that perhaps it wouldn't hurt and might even be a topic for my next book.

This rehab turned out to be the most difficult and excruciating twenty-eight days of my life, and of course I didn't write a book and actually haven't written a book since — and I'm quite happy about it. But I did write about twenty pages of a personal inventory, and I cried a lot. Now, up to this time I had written fifteen books, and this little twenty-page inventory was by far the most important thing I'd ever written in my life. It was here, in this rehab, that I was finally steered in the direction of AA thinking, and I was very scared — much more scared than before because I realized how insidious alcoholism is. And since I was returning to Poland almost immediately after getting out of the rehab, I became extremely anxious and nervous. I already knew I wouldn't make it without AA. Was there AA in Poland?

Fortunately, there was. AA had been brought to Poland about thirty years before by a nonalcoholic doctor, Zbigniew Wierzbicki, who had dealt with alcoholics in Poland and gone to the United States to learn about alcoholism treatment. He learned about the success of

AA and brought the idea back to Poland, to the city of Poznan. But Dr. Wierzbicki was not an alcoholic himself, and while he participated in the meetings he couldn't transmit to Polish alcoholics what he didn't possess himself — an understanding of the disease based on the alcoholic's own personal experience. Thus the first AA group in Poland remained under the strong influence of the medical profession. This first group had many problems — it ceased and resumed its activity several times. Since the ideas contained in the Steps had never been tried before in Poland, the founders of this group, in an effort to comply with the official atheist ideology of the state, thought they would remove God from the Steps.

It was in the early 1980s, however, when a rapid expansion of AA in Poland really began. There was a surge of feeling that the AA members wanted to go for all the Steps — as they were written — and in 1982, a Provisional National Service of AA was formed. As in any other country, these formative years witnessed a series of tensions and struggles. Finally, in October 1984 the First National AA Congress took place in Poznan, and while the Provisional Service was aware of the existence of only nineteen groups countrywide, delegates of thirty-four groups came to the convention.

AA in Poland was greatly assisted by AA abroad, especially in West Germany, Finland, the United States, and Europe. The participation of foreign AA members in Polish groups helped many Polish AAs to discover the true meaning of the Steps and Traditions. A visit from a busload of AAs from Finland in 1984 was a great experience for many Polish groups, and the long-term visits to Poland by American AAs of Polish origin has enhanced our understanding of sober living. These Polish-speaking alcoholics worked with many Polish groups, sponsored newcomers, helped establish new groups, and were a living example that AA works.

AA in Poland was also greatly helped by the efforts of individual AAs within Poland — especially the efforts of one power-driven fellow in Warsaw who couldn't seem to get along with the other group members' ideas of how AA should work. This fellow knew he couldn't stay sober without AA, but when the group began resisting his drive for power and control, he packed up and started another group

. . . and another . . . and another. This guy established five groups in a little bit more than a year! He also wrote letters to all the groups before the First AA Congress, advising them not to attend the conference since it was going to be funded by sources outside AA. The groups went anyway, but the effect of his letters was that the delegates were very cautious and it was eventually decided to give back as much of the money as possible. (It was like the Rockefeller business in the United States, when the AAs of that time realized that money from outside sources could have a detrimental effect.) So, from those people even who are doing something wrong, some good will come. It was a lesson that AA once established will heal itself.

The most important reason why there was so much growth in the early nineteen-eighties was clearly that it came after the Solidarity move-ment in Poland, which spread the idea that people could try self-help organizing for themselves. Before, the alcoholics in Poland were looking up to the medical profession, looking for somebody else to come and help them. In the eighties, though, the idea of self-help was reinforced by eco-nomic realities: people had to help each other just to survive.

AA has also been gaining support of the two most powerful institu-tions in Polish life: the Communist State and the Catholic Church. In Poland the state controls almost all institutions and organizations, includ-ing police, courts, radio and television, hospitals and treatment centers, while the Catholic Church holds control over the majority beliefs.

Though the state and the church are often in conflict, one to another, they share a concern about alcoholism and the desire to do something about it, but the acceptance of AA ideas required a lot of flexibility on the part of both these institutions. Yet state officials, policemen, judges, probation officers — as well as Catholic clergymen — seeing the many human miracles who return to sanity in Alcoholics Anonymous, treated AA with growing interest and respect.

During the last few years there has also been a widespread effort among AAs in Poland to cooperate with the press, and this has pushed the spread of the AA message well beyond the familiar person-to-per-son range, so that AA is better and better known throughout the country. There have been many stories about AA in the press — which is wholly owned either by the state or the church — and quite a number of radio programs featuring alcoholism and AA. There was also an hour-long television transmission of an actual AA meeting — without showing any faces — something which could never be done in the United States since somebody would have to pay for it.

Since its beginning, the AA movement in Poland has been closely connected to professionals, and in the spirit of cooperation, this partnership is being continued in various forms. With the help of doctors and psychologists, therapeutic/educational groups come into being, out of which, after some period of "ripening," independent AA groups emerge, and professionals systematically direct their patients to already existing AA groups. Particular groups also cooperate with dispensaries for alcoholics and alcoholic wards in hospitals. AA in Poland also maintains close contacts with the Psychoneurological Institute in Warsaw, the assistance of which enabled organization of the First AA Congress. It can only be hoped that all this publicity and help will bear fruit in the future, for the existing 200 groups in Poland today can reach only a tiny fraction of the alcoholics in Poland who need such help.

While the Steps and Traditions are precisely the same in Poland as they are everywhere else, the meetings are somewhat different. We don't have very many speaker meetings, and there is also very little AA literature. The "Twelve and Twelve" was translated three years ago, and we now have the book *Living Sober* which has been translated into Polish. What people would do is work the Steps at the meetings. Also the meetings in Poland would always begin with the question, "Does anyone here have an urgent personal problem?" and usually someone did. In the United States, at the meetings I attended, people rarely get into the very personal matters of sex and the details of family arguments and quarrels. Part of that is because AA is more than fifty years old in the U.S., and there are sponsors and AAs can talk about those kind of things on a one-to-one basis. But in Poland there weren't that many people sober long enough to really serve as sponsors. Of course people meet and talk on an individual basis, but it is not really a recognized part of the program. In Poland, your group is your sponsor. It's like — in a metaphorical sense — when you tell just one person about your problems, they metaphorically then share fifty percent of your burden. However, if there are twenty people in the group then everyone takes five percent and I have only five percent left to carry by myself. So while there is certainly a need for speakers meetings — for nonalcoholics, professionals, family members and prospective AAs to get more information about AA — the bulk of the meetings in Poland are in-depth discussion meetings.

In 1984, a series of contact points was established in Warsaw and other cities — telephone answering services, essentially — and these contact points were announced on radio and in the press. This produced a great wave of inquiries and new members, and there was some fear that with so many people coming in there would not be enough people with two or three years' sobriety to effectively pass on the message. Thus, at one time, we were putting fewer announcements in the press for fear that the structure of the groups would collapse.

The structure in Poland starts with the groups, and each group sends two delegates to the National Service Congress, which meets every two years. It had forty people a few years ago, and over two hundred and fifty now. And they all come together and select the Board of Trustees, known as "the Seven" — who are AA members from all over Poland. And the Congress also makes the crucial decisions for AA as a whole. The trustees meet every two months, and these meetings are open to all alcoholics. In the future Poland will probably have a Board of Trustees comprised of alcoholics and nonalcoholics, but this has not happened yet.

One area of concern will be for the trustees to establish an independent legal corporation, separate from both the church and the state, which will be empowered to publish its own literature. So far, Poland has been dependent on AA literature published in other countries. And, while the international help has been tremendous, Poland must soon become self-sufficient. The last National Congress of delegates, held in September 1987, resolved to legally incorporate the National Service. The most feasible form of this will be the establishment of the Alcoholics Anonymous Foundation in Poland.

The basic thing for the future of AA in Poland will be the translation of the Big Book, which is currently being worked on, and which will hopefully be published in Poland if AA can establish a separate corporation.

We had a lot of conflicts — different factions and frictions — and we Poles, we like to fight and struggle, and I must say that the conflicts usually turned out to be very productive. By conflict we grew as a Fellowship, and whenever people complain about conflicts, I can only think of the struggles of AA in America as described in *AA Comes of Age*. Out of conflict comes growth and the ability to carry the AA message more effectively.

Wiktor O.
(January 1988)

AA Pioneers

Kristiansand, Norway

April 7, 1997, marked AA's fiftieth anniversary in Norway. The event was celebrated with candlelit closed meetings all over the country. Two larger celebrations were held in May, one official and one internal for AA members. At the official celebration in Oslo, AAs met the officials of Norway, including the minister of social affairs, and the media. There were speeches and entertainment. Two days later, AA members assembled at a conference in Beitostolen. The theme was "Faith, Hope, and Victory."

How it began in Norway

In 1946 there lived a modest Norwegian, George, in Greenwich, Connecticut. He had emigrated from Norway some years earlier and owned a coffeeshop. He was an alcoholic, but he had gotten sober in AA in the early forties. Then he heard that his brother Fredrik in Norway was having great problems with alcohol, and George decided to help him. He sold his coffeeshop and together with his wife returned to Oslo to help his brother. It was very difficult to get his brother sober and even harder to get him to understand what AA was about. George almost gave up when his wallet was nearly empty. But just before he went back to the United States, his brother asked him for a meeting list. Fredrik said he saw at least a hope of reaching what had gotten his brother sober. He was beginning to understand what AA was all about. George had planted a seed, but had to go back to the States and didn't personally see the concrete results of his work.

Fredrik advertised in a newspaper and after a while he met Gunnar, who grabbed the message of AA with desire. They started working, and George sent some literature from AA headquarters in New York. At about the same time there were some patients at a health clinic a short distance from Oslo who started a club of friends. Three of the members, Arnold, Gustav, and Erling, wanted to find a permanent solution to their alcohol problem, and they read some AA literature. When they came back to Oslo, they came in contact with Fredrik and Gunnar, and on April 7, 1947, these five men started the first AA group in Norway. They called the group Janus 2.

At about the same time something was happening in another Norwegian town, Bergen on the west coast. It was developing without any connection or knowledge of what was happening in Oslo. Hans had many years of alcohol problems behind him in the spring of 1946. He met a seaman at a clinic where he was for the second time. This seaman gave Hans some pamphlets he had gotten in New York. Hans read the material with great interest and contacted AA headquarters in New York and got more literature. At this time he worked alone, but after a while he met three men who had heard of AA at a clinic. Together they started the first group in Bergen, in March 1948. They called their group Anoal.

PERIOD OF GROWTH

After some time, several groups were started in Oslo and Bergen. The members in the two towns learned about each other. At the first anniversary on April 7, 1948, they took a survey and found that AA membership in Norway was 200. Most of the members lived in Oslo and Bergen, but after a while the movement spread over the whole country. The first AA members in Norway worked very hard to spread the message in contact work, group meetings, and information meetings. They traveled around and started groups in different towns.

A great thing happened in 1950: Bill W. visited Norway. His visit was a strong stimulus to AA here and the source of great publicity. In a few years the total number of groups reached sixty, and the movement was mentioned positively by the press. Information meetings, press conferences, and radio interviews were held. But everything was not idyllic. The pioneers were flying blind, trying and failing as they debated questions of money, prestige, and anonymity. Self-support was a new concept in Norway. We sought and got economic support from outside institutions, including the government. But the pioneers in Norway contacted the headquarters in New York and took the stand that AA has to base its activity on its own economic resources. Since then self-support has been just as important as anonymity.

As clinics were established around the country, alcoholism treatment improved. Many AA members, as private persons, went into the work to establish more clinics.

AA membership grew rapidly in the fifties. Although AA kept no records, we read from newspaper articles that AA had 5,000 members.

Building a service structure

Gradually, an AA service structure was formed. A monthly magazine began as well as a board for the whole country. The first meeting was held in Stavanger in 1951. In the seventies, the first service conferences with delegates from the whole country were held. The structure in Norway included committees at different levels.

It was not before 1970 that AA in Norway got a service office. In the beginning it was run by volunteers, but in 1990 it acquired a paid staffer with an office in Oslo.

Today we have about 2,000 AA members in twenty regions which work for the common interest. Membership should be higher. Alcoholism is one of the biggest problems in Norway. This is our challenge.

Thor W.
(October 1997)

'A HARD SPIRITUAL LABOR'

Krasnodar, Russia

lcoholics Anonymous reached our city, Krasnodar, situated in South Russia a few miles to the north of the Black Sea, in 1993. We now have a six-year history of liberating people from alcohol addiction following the Twelve Steps. Our group, Sissitia, consists of twelve participants. In our city of 700,000 people we have a few anonymous alcoholics, but the number of those who still can't give up this charming practice is overwhelming. We can bring the horse to water, but we can't make it drink. This proverb illustrates the attempts of the AA movement to expand in our region. We make ourselves known in all the mass media, people come, listen, and go back to the delirium of getting drunk and getting into trouble. We can only hope that the horse will someday find its way back to the place where it once tasted clear water.

I don't think our meeting room is the best you can find, but you can't take it for an opium den either: four windows, a tall ceiling, curtains, tables, and chairs. This much of a rental fee we can afford. The samovar is electric but with porcelain cups. According to the Tradition stating that every group has to be independent, we try to stay within the boundaries of our budget.

We can really talk about each Step for a long time and with a lot of trust, since we want to understand the meaning, direction, and contents of spiritual progress. This helps us stay sober. In the past, a face to face conversation always consisted of three ingredients: a minimum of two people and as big a bottle of strong liquor as we could find. Now, entering the AA meeting room, I see people who understand what I want to say with a half-uttered word or a glance. That's why a candid conversation starts right away, without any tension. We don't know the proper way to hold meetings, but they attract with their frankness and novelty. I'm fully convinced that God for me is sobriety; every day I pray to obtain it, and ask my higher power for help.

I think that the AA movement in our country has taken the right path. Yes, we do have certain difficulties; we are few, we are poor, as only alcoholics can be, but we are gradually coming to understand that sobriety is a hard spiritual labor that lasts every day and all through life. In our country, alcoholics are socially vulnerable; they don't earn a big income (even when educated), because due to the constant consuming of poor quality alcohol, they simply cannot use the capacities of their minds. I hope that as we enroll in the AA way, we will learn to stay sober, regain our abilities, learn to earn money and invest it partly in the AA groups. We'll become a community of sensible people, and every newcomer who joins us will be able to see with his own eyes the results of spiritual work and will be less scared to start a sober life.

If we look into the future we can clearly see that technical progress will affect the AA movement. Virtual AA meetings will certainly be in fashion, and if you take into account how fast the Twelve Steps are spreading, the meetings will probably be continuous, and every time we want to drink, we'll turn on the computer and talk to a group we are interested in talking to. Virtual meetings will enable us to perceive each other on the basis of democracy and loyalty. In Russia today, letters, going by trains and airplanes, take more time to get to their destination than when they were transported by horses. It's one of our peculiarities, moreover, that very often letters get lost and never reappear. So having a dialogue with others via E-mail is very important. When you have an irresistible desire to get drunk, that always appears when you least expect it, you want to talk to somebody. Talking over a computer to Jean or Steve or Tom keeps you from going to the nearest bar. Maybe a formula that once saved an alcoholic on Cape Cod will appear on the screen as he shares it with the rest of the world, and somebody in faraway Russia will stay sober for one more day.

Looking into my mailbox, I feel joy every time I find a gift from the United States there: an illustrated magazine with a glossy cover — the Grapevine. Reading it, I study English, but still wish I could get it in Russian. Maybe someday I'll be able to get the magazine through the Internet, copy it onto a diskette, get a line by line translation, and the process of digesting information will go a lot faster. Some articles that will be especially interesting could be stored and used in a sober life. The more we communicate, using all the contemporary devices, the better we will understand each other, going deeply into the peculiarities of being an alcoholic in another country. Let's communicate as often as possible with the help of letters, phone calls, magazines, the Internet, or whatever else we can come up with: our sobriety will benefit from it.

Valery M.
(January 2000)

Part Four

Loners

LETTERS ARE MY LIFELINE

Marondera, Zimbabwe

If anyone had told me I could be alone but not lonely in the heart of Africa, I would not have believed them.

My parents are both alcoholics. My father made it in AA, my mother did not. But I grew up believing that I could handle alcohol, even if my parents could not.

Then my parents left Zimbabwe and went to live in England. The restraints were gone. It took only three years for me to graduate from a sometimes careless social drinker to a full-blown alcoholic.

I had a terrifying vision of becoming like my mother, who was one of the living dead. My blackouts were increasing; my family was falling apart. One day sitting on the porch in the warm African sun (with a hangover), I could see a tunnel — long and black with no light at the end. With trembling fingers I dialed the AA number in the phone book.

A soft Scottish-accent voice answered. The next Sunday I made the trip into Harare, forty miles away, to visit the AA woman I'd spoken to on the phone. I wasn't too sure at first that this would be the answer, but the following week I went in again, stayed the night with her, and went to my first AA meeting.

How many times since have I heard the words, "It was like coming home." At the meeting, I was just Liz, not anyone's wife, mother, daughter, or aunt. Just Liz. I started going to meetings every second Friday night and staying over. I deliberately blocked the thought of my husband's growing resentment at being left to look after three children.

There was another aspect of it, too. As much as I loved AA, I felt like an outsider, always looking in with my nose pressed on the window pane. Members were friends with each other, they'd arrive and leave together, make social dates with each other, talk about conventions, trips, and special speakers. It seemed that all the best things happened when I couldn't be there.

I learned so much — all head knowledge. It hadn't reached my heart. I could talk the talk as they say, but my resentment blocked me from being able to walk the walk.

After about six months I started to drink again, just a little I thought. I was genuinely surprised when my husband noticed, and said that AA wasn't working, so I couldn't go anymore. I replied angrily that if I couldn't go, I would just drink on Friday nights instead.

This was when I learned that alcoholism is a progressive disease. The following year was the blackest year of all. Finally a concerned and loving priest took me into Harare, to meet with an AA woman he had contacted. It turned out to be the Scottish woman. She gave me a copy of the *Loners-Internationalists Meeting* bulletin — *LIM*. I wasn't sure it would work, but I had nothing to lose. The idea of writing to people fascinated me. I'd always loved writing. So I nervously wrote to the General Service Office in New York. It wouldn't have surprised me if no one answered, but I didn't drink for two weeks, waiting for a reply. The response from GSO was warm and loving and so was the first letter from a Loner sponsor. I figured I would stay on the wagon just a little longer. And more letters came, people writing to me. It was unbelievable. Every time *LIM* arrived, I would write to five or six new listed Loners, and Loner sponsors. And I stayed sober (or was it just dry?).

Somewhere along the line the dryness became sobriety. A new chapter began: making long distance friends. Some letter-writers remained as acquaintants, some faded out, and some developed into real friendships. I wrote to people all over the world, good friends I now had in some strange sounding places. Basically though, it was the Americans that responded with a warmth and generosity I'd never known. One friend in particular has become a household word in our home. He sends books, articles, tapes, all manner of things that bring such a rich dimension to my life. He's a friend I can say anything to, sharing strength, hope, and experience as well as pain and joy. I have learned so much.

Three and a half years later and my vigor for writing letters hasn't faded. It has often been my lifeline. So many times a letter has arrived at just the right moment, with just the right words for a situation in my life.

I now go out socially more than I ever have in my life. Often I will sit and write a long letter in the afternoon. This somehow strengthens my resolve, and reinforces my thinking in a positive way. In our small, somewhat old-fashioned and backward community, most of our new social circle doesn't know that I am an alcoholic, and I can relax and enjoy myself, knowing that I've been talking to a friend in AA in a letter that very afternoon.

I write at least one letter almost every day of my life. In a very real way, I experience more meetings in a small African town than those who live in the capital city.

Recently I attended an AA conference in Harare. Some of us shared and talked about how it can be so easy just to attend two or three meetings a week, listen to a drunkalog, and then do nothing for the rest of the week. Some had slipped and some had gone back out.

I can see how easily I could have fallen into that trap, had it not been for letters and reading a lot of AA literature. In letters we often discuss what Step we're on and how to go about living the AA program in all our affairs.

I can see now how very much I have to be grateful for, when in the beginning, my resentment at my inability to get to AA meetings almost destroyed me.

L. G.
(September 1988)

ALONE? NOT THIS LONER!

Salisbury, Rhodesia

y definition, a Loner is a person who practices the AA program without the benefit of live discussions and active membership in an AA group. The designation does not mean that he is alone.

Since most of my four and a half years in AA have been spent away from a group, I am listed as a Loner. When I first returned to the Bundu after only two weeks in AA, I thought it would be impossible to manage on my own. Little did I realize then that this wouldn't be the case. The assumption that being unable to attend meetings meant going it alone was entirely wrong. At first, being registered at the AA General Service Office as a Loner didn't mean a thing to me. But when the first batch of letters arrived from overseas, it was brought home to me that there were other people in the world who were concerned about my sobriety and were willing to help me, through correspondence.

It soon became obvious that to avoid the danger of that first drink I had to keep myself fully occupied, and I had to look around for new hobbies to fill the time I now had on my hands, since it was no longer expended on finding new hiding places for my supplies and on digging up the wherewithal to buy them!

It was also apparent that social life on a small station would prove difficult at times, since the others there all seemed to enjoy their drinking, and most of the station activities took place in and around the club. The fact that the rest of the world was not going to come to a standstill because I happened to be an alcoholic was another factor that had to be taken into account. Later, very much later, I was to discover that at official functions, of which there were many, nobody bothered themselves about what I drank, as long as I had a glass of something in my hand. It was a bit disconcerting to find that another of my old excuses for drinking was really unfounded!

It has often been remarked by members of AA groups that they couldn't possibly stay sober under such circumstances. This is sheer nonsense! You can do anything you really and truly want to do. The expression "I could not bear it" is another fallacy. Of course you can bear it if you really want to remain sober, but any excuse is good enough if you are looking for an excuse to drink again.

Once I had recovered physically, I found that being a Loner was a far-from-lonely life. Soon my circle of friends-through-correspondence grew larger and larger, and time never hung heavy, because there was always the anticipation of what the mail would bring, and then there were the letters to answer.

The AA who sits at home and makes himself miserable because he has no contacts has only himself to blame, and is heading for trouble. To be happily sober, we must be active — and this does not necessarily mean group activity. The Loner is part of a much larger group of people in far distant places, all members of AA with the same problems, fears, and happiness to be shared. And what could be more exciting than making friends all over the world? There is also the new medium of communication through taping. Just watch a "tapeworm" grab his mail, sort through it till he finds a tape, and rush home to his tape recorder to listen to a voice which has come to mean much to him, though it belongs to someone he has never met and is not likely to meet. Then you will see what I mean.

Apart from these correspondents by letter and tape, the only person with whom I could discuss AA matters was my husband, and at times he must have been bored to tears listening to me, though he was patience personified and never showed his boredom.

When someone says, "I admire you for the courage you have shown in remaining sober on your own," I feel a twinge of guilt, because I have never really been on my own. I may not be in face-to-face contact with other AA members, but my real friends in AA are too many to enumerate, and I find there aren't enough hours in the day to do all I should do.

So to GSO, to the bulletin *Loners-Internationalists Meeting*, the Grapevine, World Hello, and all the other publications, and to other Loners and Loner sponsors who have helped me to stay sober, I am deeply indebted. Keep up the good work, and thank you all.

W. H.
(February 1970)

The Only AA Member Writes From Indonesia

Jakarta, Indonesia

Here in Indonesia, the land of the sun and monsoon rains, I am the only AA member. My name is Mary. We came here in September 1959 from Tucson, Arizona, where I had been a member of a fine and wonderful group for over two years. With what an aching heart and grave misgivings I left Tucson to become a Loner. And how fortunate for me I had had good indoctrination into AA by the ever helpful and friendly members in Tucson. If my basic teachings had been less effective, I wonder if I'd still be sober as of this writing. However, I know I don't want to go back into that bottomless pit of agony. I want to stay sober. The fact that I wanted to find a way to stop drinking and discovered that AA was my only recourse (after the usual thousands of promises that I'd quit drinking or go on the wagon — which I succeeded in doing for three days once — or only drink weekends, etc.) was undoubtedly of great benefit. For as I had lapped up liquor previously so now did I lap up every word I heard in AA and was able, thank God, to retain some of the teachings when I came out here.

Being a member of an AA group is a wonderful thing, and it is exceedingly hard to leave. The transition has not been easy. When I suddenly found myself unable to see or talk to another AA, I realized how fortunate I'd been. I cannot in all honesty say that I have been completely happy as a Loner nor can I say it hasn't been worthwhile. But one can make things as easy or as hard for oneself as one wants. In my stupid way I have done both. When the days seem to drag on, long and wearisome, I know that is when my armor is down, my thinking bad, and my resentments come to the fore. Then I realize I'm not working the program the way I should. I've forgotten to live it a day at a time. So back onto the twenty-four-hour program I leap and things become easy once more, just living the program as best I can. There are also times when I've felt I could not stand it another minute without my group or any group, and the craving to see and talk to them is overwhelming. When this feeling persists I write to members of my group, hold meetings by myself (you'd be surprised how beneficial that is), read more of the Big Book. And then, feeling the program, I no longer seem physically alone and the violent longing passes from me.

I miss Twelfth Step work a great deal. Indonesia is a Moslem state and the Moslem religion prohibits the use of alcohol. However, the natives are not all abstemious. Having found out there is a drinking problem amongst them as well as the foreign element, I've asked ministers, doctors and priests of different nationalities if they knew of anyone wanting help. As yet no takers. After I ran an ad in the local English-speaking paper, I was warned not to try to cross the language barrier and run one in the Indonesian papers as well. For reasons I don't understand the Indonesian-owned English paper suddenly refused to run my ad any longer except at an exorbitant price. It has been suggested to me that as this is a military as well as Moslem country (stretching for some 3,000 miles and a thousand islands across the Java Sea from Sumatra, Java, Borneo and the Celebes to New Guinea), maybe the hint in the paper that there was an alcoholic problem here was not well received by the officials. So my attempts at recruiting have not been fruitful so far.

On the other hand, being a loner has taught me things I am sure I might never have learned otherwise. I have been blessed with a wonderful sponsor, Jeanne H. of Tucson, whose constant understanding, love, and constructive criticism have been a lifeline to me in some of my trials and struggles with myself out here. Happily a phone call from Jakarta to the States costs very little. Most long distance calls are placed from the local phone company office. Sometimes it takes five or six days to get a call through. When waiting to get a call through I have practically lived at the office. Because of weather conditions sometimes the only hour I can get through is 5:30 a.m., Tucson time. Never once has Jeanne complained. She has always seemed glad to hear from me, though sometimes we sound as though we were either under water or gargling. It goes without saying that after hearing her cheery voice I return home greatly exhilarated and feel as though a weight has been lifted from my shoulders. Her many and faithful letters have shown me what a true sponsor and friend she is. I doubt if until now I really appreciated my wealth in her friendship.

Thanks to GSO, an AA member, working on a ship, found out about my being here and we had a fine get-together last fall. He in turn told Dick D. in Singapore about me and Dick immediately wrote me. Since then we have kept up a continuous correspondence. My husband and I are going to Singapore in a few months and then at last I will meet Dick and go to a long-awaited meeting. Dick spread the word, as did GSO, that I was here and I have received letters from all over the world — from Australia to Copenhagen and from one end of Canada and the United States to the other. I cannot tell you how wonderful it is to know so many persons are happy to give their time and themselves to a Loner. In what other organization would you find such friendliness, good cheer and concern over a total stranger! The interesting thing is that I don't feel like a stranger with them. We know all about our struggles and lives before and after AA. There is a great bond through correspondence as well as through physical contact. And the Tucson Group writes me faithfully — bless them. Other groups from all over the world have generously sent me their bulletins which I pour over as avidly as I do the Grapevine. Sometimes when reading these pamphlets I even read where their meetings are to take place and the time and dates, though of course I have no idea what their city or town looks like. It gives me a nice close feeling of being in touch.

I find I read more AA literature than ever before. Each afternoon I do some reading. I have nothing much else to do although I take Indonesian lessons and have an English conversation group for Indonesian women eager to learn. In my spare time I study the AA literature carefully because I want to and I need to. When in the group, I did not feel I needed to. Now I know how wrong I was. I think we all need to, or can it be possible that I'm the only one who sort of slid over a lot of it after the first initial plunge of absorption and eagerness? I wonder.

By chance, at the time of my third anniversary, we took a trip to the island of Bali, just east of Java where we live. What a romantic and beautiful place! Most of my anniversary was spent walking across verdant, waving green rice paddies; through an ancient monkey temple (monkeys, scampering about holding coconuts, are the only ones allowed to enter parts of the temple); and in mountain villages where we were the only visitors. The quiet stillness of the vast, tiered rice fields, the chattering of the monkeys blending with the singing of the birds in this tropical jungle, added zest to my elation and thankfulness for having made my anniversary. I could not have asked for more. And when I returned to Jakarta, I found a birthday card from the Tucson Group with all their signatures!

Most fortunately for me, I found out early on that I needed something more than the group as my Higher Power and so I had God, as I understood him, to guide me. I am sure he helped me make my anniversary, although as Jeanne wrote me, knowing I was getting jittery, "Remember it's just another day in our day-to-day life." I am most grateful to AA for having shown me that God is a loving God, and no longer do I fear him as I did all my life. I know definitely, after having been here these many months, that he is always with me, guiding me, soothing me and uplifting me. I could not for a long time believe that it was God's will that I come out here. I'd fought coming out here as I was so scared I'd drink again and be lost once more. I did not have enough faith or confidence. However, I now do have faith that it was his will. Maybe the only reason, for there is always a reason, was to point out to me how much more I needed him than I had thought, that I could always depend on him, and that once I became a Loner I would gain through faith and prayer the strength and fortitude I need to see myself as I really am. In a physical sense I may be a Loner but never am I alone spiritually. For all this I am deeply grateful.

M. H.
(October 1960)

A WHOLE NEW OUTLOOK ON LIFE

Dar es Salaam, Tanzania

There is an old African legend that whenever an ostrich sees the outbreak of a savanna bushfire likely to destroy its brood or its eggs, the only precaution it cares to take is to bury its head in the ground. It does so in the pretense that "if I cannot see the fire, then the fire cannot destroy me." But the reality remains; when the fire spreads and finds the ostrich unprepared, it sweeps away the whole family, including the unprotected eggs and chicks.

In the first full year that I've been able to stay sober through the AA program, I have come to regard the behavior of us drunks as being like that of the ostrich.

During the twenty-four years of my hard-drinking career, I ventured blindly through the jungle of life, refusing to face its reality, for fear that it would ruin me if I did face it. Instead, it ruined me because I didn't have the courage to face it. The more I drank, the more I needed to drink, so as to shut out the slightest light coming from the dreadful reality of life.

Years rolled by, and the changes brought about by time passed by unnoticed. Not until I was in the darkest fog of booze, not until I had lost nearly everything of value, did I hear a faraway call, telling me that I had to do something about my drinking, or else.

The call came in the form of some AA literature given to me by an expatriate fellow worker, who guessed my drinking problem as soon as he set eyes on me. He also allowed me to go through his copy of the Big Book. Although I found the literature and the philosophy contained therein very convincing, I just couldn't stomach the idea that AA was for me. I still prided myself on my willpower, which had earlier saved me in a lot of other situations. I thought, "It is only a matter of time before I will drop the drinking habit and return to my normal self." So I kept cheating myself.

Everything came to a standstill after the sudden death of my dear mother. She had held the fort for me during my twenty-four-year absence from the reality of life. Now, no matter how much I tried to blind my mind with booze, some light managed to filter in, and it illuminated the true state of affairs: The bushfire was mercilessly blowing toward me, destroying job, home, family life, and all the rest. Left with nowhere to run for protection, I was forced to face life squarely, with all its ups and downs. Where was I to gather the strength?

I had been born and brought up a Christian, though my faith had deteriorated gravely during my drinking. Whenever in distress, I had always found a brief moment to turn to my Higher Power, whom I believed and still believe to be Almighty God. And at no time throughout my forty-three years had I faced bigger and tougher distress than this. Now, I had no one to run to except my Higher Power.

While I was saying all sorts of prayers, something clicked and reminded me of the AA literature I had discarded about five years back. I tried to recall some of the philosophy I'd come across there. Something like ". . .were powerless over alcohol, and our lives had become unmanageable" kept reappearing in my damaged mind. In desperation, I resolved to look through the discarded literature to see where I had found those words, and whether there was more where they came from. On digging through the piles of reading material, I came across an old copy of the AA Grapevine. Just inside the front cover, I found what I was looking for — the Twelve Steps. I realized that the first three Steps were made for me personally. The rest were more difficult to understand, so I decided to take more time with them later on.

Eventually, as a Loner member of AA, I found Step Twelve to have a very encouraging effect when practiced sincerely. I made a list of some of my old drinking companions here who, I felt, must have reached bottom and definitely could do with the hand of AA. I explained to them, one by one, how the program had helped me and saved my home from becoming a wreck. Most of them were and still are surprised at the way I had changed so abruptly. Without being proud of myself, I humbly noticed that I was becoming a sort of example to be followed by those who had reached a point near despair. Together, we have formed a small group, and the AA General Service Office has provided us with the important AA literature.

I am now in my second year of sobriety through the AA program.

Although not all of the problems created during the days when I hid in the fog of booze have straightened out, I now have enough courage to face them squarely. I have learned to do "First Things First," without having to escape from the truth: Most of those problems were of my own making.

L. N.
(December 1978)

———⚬———

LONER

Ponape, Caroline Islands

Living on a small tropical Pacific island a thousand miles from the nearest live AA meeting poses special problems for a recovering alcoholic. There are many rewards, however. I benefit from the AA program in coping with the island lifestyle, and I benefit from the special frame of mind that island living develops.

There is a sense of timelessness in the islands, especially in those far from the normal shipping lanes, like ours. When ships do arrive, their coming has very little relationship with any posted schedule. Even the airline, which attempts to fly on time, is at the mercy of the weather.

The working day has specific hours, but anyone who wanted to transact business at a government office during the first hour of the working day would find the majority of the desks empty. On the other hand, quitting time is religiously adhered to, with many leaving early so they won't miss it. With this attitude prevalent, Easy Does It comes naturally.

An attitude of impatience or resentment is frequently seen in the casual visitor. Adjustment is not instantaneous, but nothing is gained by trying to change the situation. Somehow, the work gets done.

This island is part of an emerging nation, which is having its share of growing pains. My work is closely involved with the operation and maintenance of the limited existing facilities, as well as the development of a system of self-government for the nation. As a result, more than a fair share of unusual problems needs attention daily. When I was still drinking, my chances of retaining my sanity in this set of circumstances would have been close to zero. However, the way I work it now is extremely simple.

As each problem reaches my desk, I try to identify its exact nature. Then, it only remains to see whether an immediate solution is available. Often, it is not apparent, in which case I ask my Higher Power for guidance or, in effect, "the wisdom to know the difference." Sometimes a solution occurs to me or to one of my employees. Sometimes none does, but if there is a course of action available, it is immediately pursued. If not, the problem is left in the hands of God as I understand him. Because of the rather indifferent attitude toward time and toward any distinction between what is urgent and what is not, in many cases the problems simply disappear.

One key to success has been the elimination from my vocabulary of the word "blame." It is all too easy to point your finger at the next person and say that he or she was the cause of the trouble. If I did this, I wouldn't have time to get anything fixed, and Lord knows, there is plenty to be fixed here.

Since the only alcoholics on the island are still practicing, and there is usually a language and culture barrier between us, I have little chance at present for Twelfth Step work. I hope this will change as I grow more proficient in the language.

By active practice of Steps Ten and Eleven, I maintain my own sobriety without much trouble. Either in the evening or in the early morning, I read the *Twenty-four Hours a Day* book. That and the Big Book are all I brought with me. Quite often, I have found that the daily meditation and prayer have been particularly appropriate to the problems of the day, and that my prayer has been heard. Promptly admitting my own mistakes (and they are many) has helped penetrate both the manager-employee barrier and the culture barrier. All I can do is attempt to set a good example and hope that my employees —

many of whom have a problem with alcohol, especially with the local island drink known in Polynesia as *kava* — will be able to benefit by my example.

Anonymity here on this island for me is a matter of degree. My feeling is that if there is any benefit in breaking my anonymity, I will. When the benefit was obvious, I have broken it with several people, and since this is an island, I'm certain that anyone who has the slightest interest knows by now that I'm an alcoholic. However, I don't try to proselytize among the local people. If any alcoholics among them are ready, they know who and where I am.

My meetings consist of the bulletin *Loners-Internationalists Meeting*, correspondence with other Loners and with Loner sponsors by letter and cassette tape, and a periodic head-to-head meeting with a German AA member employed on one of the ships that call here. I've been fortunate enough to go to Australia and attend three live meetings in the last year and a half, and have recently begun working through such organizations within AA as World Hello. I cannot emphasize enough the importance of mail to a person on an island, and when it's good AA mail, it's twice as welcome.

If anyone reading these words is contemplating a move to one of the Pacific island "paradises," he or she should be sure to bring a good working relationship to AA, remember and understand the Serenity Prayer, and be prepared to live one day at a time.

S. C. T.
(August 1976)

Part Five

Interviews

You **Can** Go Home Again

Czech Republic

l K., born in the Czech Republic, has been sober for thirty years. In 1955, he fled his native country after being released from a labor camp. Eventually he made his way to the United States, got sober in Washington, D.C., and returned to his country after the 1990 revolution. Since then, he has spent four to five months every year in the Czech Republic, helping to carry the AA message. (During the rest of the year, he divides his time between Florida and Washington.) Al was interviewed in the Grapevine offices by a member of the Grapevine's Editorial Advisory Board.

Grapevine: When did you first learn of AA?

Al: I knew about AA back in Chicago. There was a Czech priest, and I used to see him once in a while. I'd call him when I was drinking: you know how it is — you're drunk, you're kind of sobbing, and you're feeling sorry for yourself. So a couple of times when I was still drinking in Chicago, I'd call him up, let's say at two o'clock in the morning, and sob on the phone. One time he said, "So how's your drinking?" And I said, "Well, I'm doing pretty good, I'm keeping it two days apart, you know. Two or three times a week." And he said, "You know, you're so smart and at the same time you're so stupid. Why don't you go to AA?"

And years later when I was in Washington, D.C., and I was desperate, I finally called AA. So that's a little of my story.

Grapevine: When did you return to the Czech Republic?

Al: When I was fifty-five I retired, so I went back to the Czech Republic to visit. And I saw this opportunity about AA. It was 1990, and there was nothing going on there. It gave me a new purpose in life, if you will. And I had a great, great time enjoying Prague, and meeting these new people, and starting new groups. So that's why I go there

— it helps me tremendously. There's the fantastic joy of seeing somebody else get sober.

At first, I was afraid to go back to Europe. I was specifically afraid to go back to the Czech Republic. My nephew was going to be ordained as a priest in 1990 (before the revolution, priests studied underground and weren't allowed to be ordained), and my sister wanted me to go back for his ordination. Initially I told her I wasn't going to go, but then my cousin in Switzerland convinced me to do it. I went through Switzerland and through Austria to the Czech Republic. And then I started feeling safe, and I've been coming in every year. When I still had a business, I was going there for three or four weeks. But since I gave the business up, I've been going for four or five months at a time. It's a great opportunity for me.

Grapevine: What were some of your first experiences with AA when you went back?

Al: My sister has another son, who was just a devastated alcoholic. She would never write me about it, but when I came in 1990 and was with him for two minutes, I knew what was the deal. I knew he was one of us. He was an ex-boxer, and he was getting into fights with people in the city, and had been in a treatment center at least three or four times. My sister was incredibly sad about it. His story by itself is a story. So before I was leaving, I said, "Carl, listen, you and me are very much the same. I'm an alcoholic, but I'm not drinking. You're an alcoholic you know." And I said, "There are some people in Prague — we're starting AA. And these people maybe can help you." So the night before I was leaving, we were out for dinner, and everybody was drinking, of course. He was drunk but he came out as I was saying goodbye to everybody, and he asked me to get in touch with him. So I connected him with a sober guy in Prague, and he hasn't had a drink since. He's been sober eight or nine years now.

Grapevine: When did Czech-speaking AA meetings start in Prague?

Al: The Communists wouldn't let the groups be in existence before 1989. In Poland, the government somehow tolerated it — they didn't allow it, but they tolerated it — but in the Czech Republic there was no AA.

Grapevine: What were the first Czech meetings like?

Al: The first meeting was in 1990. There were a lot of people, about thirty, brought up from institutions. At first, the meeting was held in the former headquarters of the Communist Party, and as we were leaving the building, the people started throwing stuff at us. They thought we were, you know, party members. So it was an interesting experience!

As the meeting grew, we started another meeting, a Step group, and then we started a Big Book group. So now we had three groups on Monday, Wednesday, and Friday which were directly related to staying sober, and the Big Book, and the "Twelve and Twelve."

Grapevine: Did you encounter other struggles as the meetings got going?

Al: We were renting space in different churches, and any time they had an activity we weren't able to have our meeting. Sometimes this would happen all summer in some of the areas. So we were looking for our own space, and spaces in Prague are very, very hard. Some people have waited ten or fifteen years before they were able to get an apartment. Some people have waited ten or fifteen years before they were able to get a telephone. We were finally able to get a dungeon-like space. We had to remodel the office completely — put heat in, and electricity, and even floors. Now we're pretty much set. And we have a telephone! We're listed in the Yellow Pages. We have an answering machine. So we have progressed, you know, substantially.

Grapevine: Were the people going to meetings trying to get sober or had they been sober for a while?

Al: Most of the people came from institutions. Lately, we're starting to get people from the street because they're learning about us. In the beginning, the treatment centers in Prague were not really helpful. They were kind of afraid of us. I think that they saw a competition in AA. Because what was happening was there was a transformation from state-sponsored medicine, doctors being paid a salary from the state, to a situation where a lot of the doctors were charging patients directly. Especially the psychologists and the psychiatrists saw in us something that could take their business away from them. Now, some of the institutions are supporting us and are sending people into a group on Tuesday.

As far as cities outside of Prague are concerned, AA is really at the very, very beginning. I started a group in my hometown actually. And the way we started that group was through my nephew who was the priest. I gave him the Big Book, and I said, "Hey, if you run into somebody who might need AA, I'll be glad to talk to him." And the next year he said, "Uncle, look, I have this guy who wants to talk to you." I said, "What's the deal?" He said, "Well, I was burying his mother and he fell into the grave three times. We pulled him out of the grave three times, and I gave him the Big Book, and he wants to talk to you." So this is how we started that group — by talking to someone one-on-one. This guy's got three years now. When he had three months, I gave him the keys to the meeting room, and said, "You are it. Just keep coming here every Wednesday, and if nobody shows up, just read the book." I keep in touch with him on the telephone. He's kind of holding the fort.

Grapevine: How many AA members are in the Czech Republic?

Al: Right now about eighty.

Grapevine: And are there many young people who've gotten sober there?

Al: We have several young people in their twenties.

Grapevine: Is there long-term sobriety in your groups?

Al: Eight or nine years, max. There are some people with five years, and there are some people with three years, and there are some people with one year and six months, and some very, very new people.

We do get a lot of repeats. They come out of institutions, and they come to meetings, and everything is nice. And then they don't need the meetings, and the God stuff is a problem to them, their spirituality is a problem for them. So next thing is you know, they get beaten up, and some of them come back. And then they do it again.

Grapevine: Do you think many people know about AA?

Al: No, very few people know about AA. Remember the Czech Republic lived over forty years in the Communist regime. People were taught materialistic, Communist, atheistic doctrine in schools, and most people would have nothing to do with God or spirituality. So that is a big issue for Czechs, you know. They need to overcome that.

Grapevine: At what rate do you think AA is growing in the Czech Republic?

Al: Very slowly. We had a great growth in Prague in the last seven years — great growth. But it's the other cities really that I'm concentrating on. I have a car there and I drive two or three hours to a meeting. There's one guy, and he and I sometimes drive three hours to a meeting, and then there's nobody there. I've waited outside on the sidewalk many times. But it doesn't bother me. I would like to see more people coming in, but I figure it will happen. And if it doesn't happen, it doesn't happen, but we just do what we can, and see what comes up.

Grapevine: Is there any message you would like to give from AA in the Czech Republic?

Al: One of the things I would like to say is that a lot of times when people put a dollar in the basket, they don't understand what the New York office is doing in terms of helping groups internationally. It [AA World Services] has translated six or seven different booklets for us. The Big Book was already translated, but they printed it for us. And they're supplying these things to the Czech Republic free of cost. So when somebody puts a dollar in the basket, it's really being used, and we're getting this kind of support in terms of literature. It's just fantastic.

(January 2000)

'ANOTHER PART OF THE ELEPHANT'

Auckland, New Zealand

In October 1998, the World Service Meeting was held in Auckland, New Zealand, with participation by thirty-nine delegates representing twenty-two countries. In August, Simon R., a second-year delegate from the host country, talked to the Grapevine by telephone and E-mail about the WSM, AA development in New Zealand, and the role of service in his recovery from alcoholism.

Simon: Perhaps one of the first service jobs I got was when a relatively new group voted me in as their secretary. With two or three years' sobriety, I was an old-timer. I was so unused to being trusted that I made another member of the group hold onto the keys. I thought that if the place got burgled they'd blame me for sure. So I used to take this lady to the meeting each Thursday and she would unlock the door, but once inside I was the secretary!

Grapevine: What were your other early service commitments?

Simon: I remember the first time I ever went to intergroup, I and another guy went to "overthrow the hierarchy" over some matter which I can't now remember. But when we got there we sat and listened for a while before we made our move. It dawned on me that they weren't just "talking business." They were trying to figure out how to better carry the message. They were talking about things that really mattered to me. I loved it when our office phone rang me with a Twelfth Step job, and I finally connected the after-hours phone calls I loved to get and this bunch of GSRs with their group donations to pay for the office, the meeting lists, the literature, and the phones!

My next service job in AA was being the after-hours phone contact, and that job was the catalyst for so much growth in my sobriety. I formed friendships that still exist today. I got involved with sponsorship and other areas of service, went to more meetings, and learned an awful lot about twelfth-stepping. I rotated off that job after fifteen months when I became a GSR and became a regular attendee at intergroup and area assemblies. What a learning ground! Sometimes I got discouraged by the seeming disunity. But it helped when I realized that all we were usually arguing about was how to better carry the message to the sick alcoholic. My own behavior bothered me too. I knew I lacked the maturity, calmness, clear thinking, and experience that I saw in some older members, but the only way to grow up is to grow up and not run away. So I didn't stop going. I found out that there is life after embarrassment, you can disagree without being disagreeable, and after a while I reached for humility as something I wanted, rather than something that happens to me at the hands of my perceived enemies. That stuff may not sound like it has much to do with service, but that is where I found it out.

Grapevine: So you decided to stay involved in service and ended up as a World Service Meeting delegate?

Simon: It seems stupid now, but as a GSR I had always been slightly suspicious of those AAs who went to our annual General Service Conference. Sure, they brought back information and seemed pretty knowledgeable, but it still looked like a scam to me. So when I was nominated for, and elected as a Conference delegate, one of the reasons I accepted was so I could expose this waste of Fellowship funds.

What a surprise I got. We arrived on the Friday night and went straight into a committee meeting. Same thing all day Saturday and a workshop Saturday night! More business Sunday morning, a rush to the airport and home to report to the people who sent me there.

Those three years on the Conference may have been busy, but they were three of the best years of my life up until then. Admittedly, I sometimes hid in service at the expense of my recovery, but no harm came to me, and I met people who taught me a lot. Some of them have passed on, and some are still with us, at assemblies and conventions, no longer holding office, but quietly instilling confidence with their presence.

Sometimes I have been a legend in my own mind. I remember once when I was suffering from this problem, my sponsor asked me, "If you leave AA tomorrow, do you know what they will say about you in six months' time?" I said I didn't know. He said, "Simon who?"

When I rotated off as a Conference delegate, I got a job as tape man at my home group and greeter at another meeting. It has always been a help to me to have more than one reason to be going to a meeting.

After three or four years I was honored to be elected as alternate World Service delegate for two years. There was not a lot of actual work in this job, but it meant that I had to keep informed, up-to-date, and attend all assemblies.

At the end of that two years, I was elected as World Service delegate. It was indeed a great honor to be elected to such a position by people whom you respect, bearing in mind of course that sometimes it's just your turn.

The senior delegate was a great help and encouraged me a lot. But really, nothing could have prepared me for what I saw, felt, and experienced in New York at my first World Service Meeting in 1996. I kept a diary while I was there, and one day's entry just reads "A day beyond my wildest dreams." That's pretty much it.

Grapevine: As a delegate, what are your major responsibilities?

Simon: I am responsible to those that elected me to the position. That means I must take or make the time to attend World Service Meetings, national conferences, and local assemblies. I should be as prepared as I can be to report to and from those meetings. That means I should be informed. If there is an agenda, I should know what is on it and be prepared to speak knowledgeably on issues that may be raised. By speaking knowledgeably I don't mean just my own opinion or experience, although they may be useful. I mean being aware of the Traditions, Concepts, and guidelines in relation to a topic. These are not hidden or secret, they are easily found in our literature. I think I also owe it to the Fellowship to ask God for guidance when participating in service, rather than just relying on myself.

Grapevine: Are there any interesting preparations under way for the World Service Meeting?

Simon: During the course of the WSM, delegates and their partners will experience a Maori cultural performance group.

Grapevine: Is there a strong participation of indigenous people in New Zealand AA?

Simon: I don't think there has ever been a proportionate number of Maori in New Zealand AA. A lot of people have asked themselves and others why this is. There are certainly Maori in the Fellowship, and over the years several of them have become real AA leaders and widely respected, but, as I say, not in proportionate numbers. In recent years there has been quite a dramatic rise in the number of Maori coming to AA, but sadly they are not all staying. They seem to leave in proportionate numbers to non-Maori, however. A major reason for the rise in new Maori members is the introduction of treatment programs designed specifically for Maori. These programs place a lot of emphasis on Maori culture and heritage, and are very well received. Upon leaving treatment, clients are referred to AA as an ongoing therapy. In AA there is no emphasis on culture, heritage, or race; we meet with one common problem and one common solution. This may be unsettling to those who have only recently "discovered" their cultural identity as something to nurture and be proud of, and who associate this culture strongly with their recovery. Sometimes the new awareness and practice of the culture takes precedence over recovery and AA meetings. I believe people of all races come to AA and look for a reason to be different, but if you are looking for a difference and you are the only brown face in a room full of white ones, you don't have to look far. Maori also leave AA for the same reasons non-Maori do. However, Maori who put recovery first, and also embrace their culture, report that they have "the best of both worlds." These people tend to be busy AA members, as they are sought after as sponsors. They come to AA meetings as "Sonia" or "Ihaia" the alcoholic, not as "Sonia" or "Ihaia" the Maori who is an alcoholic. The difference gets left at the door. Sonia and Ihaia are the members who helped me write this piece. I asked them both what they think can be done so that more Maori can stay in AA. They both said, "By being a good example yourself."

Grapevine: How does the WSM strengthen the intent of the Responsibility Declaration — that the hand of AA should always be there?

Simon: There was a time when I thought that national conferences and World Service meetings were far removed from "God's firing line." But that was a very short-sighted view. Once I began to participate at those levels, I realized that the Conference is just as much in God's firing line as the most sordid spot on earth. You only have to read the reports from the WSM to realize that the decisions are directly related to ensuring that the hand of AA is there; delegates are responding to needs as expressed through an international group conscience. The meeting both initiates and inspires, often in dramatic and well-documented ways, like the latest translation done by the International Literature Fund. Or the inception of a new regional meeting such as the Asia-Oceania Service Meeting (AOSM), which was based on similar meetings in Europe and South America. This regional meeting really makes us ask ourselves if the hand of AA is here in our own "backyards." Representation at the WSM is worthwhile, but hosting the AOSM gives us the opportunity to be "GSO New York" to someone else, closer to home. Sometimes it can be far more low-key but just as effective. During the last WSM I heard the Australian delegate talking about "pink tins." These are pink containers that sit on the secretary's table and members drop in spare change, etc., over and above their normal Seventh Tradition contribution. The money is used to put AA literature in the prisons. Anyway, when I got back home I told them about these pink tins, and before you know it, there was a pink tin in most meetings. Soon after, the AA meeting in the Christchurch Women's Prison got several new Big Books, and then Rolleston Prison, and so on. The WSM is sharing experience, strength, and hope in the spirit of Step Twelve.

Grapevine: In March 1995, New Zealand and Japan helped found the AOSM, the first service meeting for AA in Pacific Rim countries. The second AOSM was held in March 1997. Could you tell us about it?

Simon: The Asia-Oceania Service Meeting began its second meeting by adopting a statement of purpose, and guidelines regarding policy, admissions, and finance. We defined the meeting's area of responsibility, and listed the countries that lie within our zone. These countries were then divided up into "neighborhood" groups, with the more established country in each group being asked to take responsibility for sponsorship in its own neighborhood. This gives sponsor countries a focus for their work. There is a very wide range of AA development within the borders of the AOSM, from countries with long-established service structures, all the way to places where AA is almost unknown. AA exists in only eleven of the twenty-five nations within New Zealand's sponsorship group.

Grapevine: How has being a World Service Meeting delegate affected your sobriety?

Simon: My sobriety is my life. As far as I was concerned, my life was over when I was nineteen years old. I looked around and I couldn't find one good thing in my life. Suicide or permanently staying in a mental hospital were the only options I could see. But AA came to that mental hospital at 6:30 p.m. on a Monday night in the form of the Hope Group, and I have not had to take my own life. I've lived outside a mental hospital free from alcohol or any other mind-altering chemical for nineteen years. Everything in my life I owe to AA and a loving God I found there. So being a WSM delegate is part of my life and my sobriety. It has enriched my life tremendously.

I read somewhere that if you stand on the beach and look out to sea you can see the horizon twenty-three or so miles away. But if you go twenty feet up the sand dunes, the horizon is a hundred miles away. Those figures may not be accurate, but you get the idea. The WSM has been my "twenty feet up the sandhills." It is the greatest honor anyone has ever done me. Many times in my sobriety I've thought to myself, "This is marvelous. If nothing else ever happens to me, this is enough." And it keeps getting better.

I remember once I was asked to do some new job in AA, and I felt a bit nervous about it. My sponsor said, "Don't worry, it's just another part of the elephant." Not being able to resist a sponsor story I asked what he meant. He told me this story. There were these four blind guys walking along a path one day, and this guy comes toward them leading an elephant. Well, they can feel the vibration of the elephant's steps and they all say, "What the hell is that!" The guy leading the elephant says, "It's an elephant." They've never seen an elephant, so they ask, "What is an elephant like?" The guy replies, "Feel it and find out." So one blind man grabs the trunk and says, "Ah. Now I know what an elephant is like. It is long and round and wrinkly." But another blind man has grabbed the ear and he says, "No it's not, it's flat and huge." The third one has the tusk, and he says, "You guys both have it wrong, an elephant is hard and smooth, and it comes to a point at the end." The last guy has flung his arms around the leg and says, "You three must be holding on to some other creature, an elephant is round like the trunk of a tree, it goes all the way to the ground, and it is connected to something enormous at the top." They were right, but none of them had the whole picture. It's just that they each had a different part of the elephant. Good story, eh?

(January 1999)

———◉———

'I Didn't Want to Drink or to Live'

Colombia, South America

María Inés E. de B. was Director of AA's Office of General Services of Colombia when she was interviewed by the Grapevine's editor of Spanish resources.

Grapevine: Tell us a bit about you and about your work at the Office of General Services.

María Inés: I've been a member of AA in Colombia for nine years. I came into the Fellowship because I was confused and worried about my drinking. From the first meeting I attended, I realized that in AA there was a solution to my problem, and even though I didn't really understand much, I felt the strength of AA, that there was hope for my future. That's why I continued attending meetings.

Since April 26, 1996 I've been the Director of the General Service Office of AA in Colombia. Prior to that, I had been working two years as Assistant of the Board.

Grapevine: What are your main duties as Director of GSO in Colombia?

María Inés: We make sure that the Office meets all its obligations: we attend the meetings of the Board of Trustees, we share with the

Committees of the Board, we organize the General Service Conference and, most importantly, we give our support to the groups and try to give strength to solitary members. We also sponsor several countries in Latin America.

Grapevine: As a woman, was it difficult for you to come into AA?

María Inés: Even though it's not the same for all women, for me it was easy because in my group Los Doce Pasos, in Envigado, there were women of the same background, women I had studied with, acquaintances from the same county, so I always felt their support, their friendship, their guidance. And they sponsored me initially, which is so crucial for a woman.

Grapevine: Is the presence of women in AA in Colombia growing? What is the percentage in relation to that of men in the Fellowship?

María Inés: At the moment women have become more conscious of their condition as alcoholics and they are showing up more at meetings. I'd say about twenty percent of the alcoholics in recovery are women.

Grapevine: Do you think there are women who don't attend meetings because there is a stigma about declaring themselves as alcoholics?

María Inés: I think the stigma has diminished over time as women get to identify the problem, as they see other friends go through the same, then they begin to lose their fear of being classified as easy women, women who cannot be a useful member of society. Women are beginning to trust the program more and they enter recovery without as many obstacles as in the past.

Grapevine: In what segment of Colombian society is alcoholism more widespread?

María Inés: I'd say it's generalized. There's alcoholism among the upper class, a little camouflaged in the social clubs and in, shall we call them, the distinguished establishments. Alcoholism has deep roots in the working class. The middle class, I think, drinks as a way of escaping their problems and their anguish. So I'd say there's alcoholism everywhere.

Grapevine: Is there more alcoholism in some areas of the country than in others?

María Inés: In the major cities there's a great concentration of alcoholics, but there is also alcoholism in rural places because of the isolation and inactivity and lack of other forms of distraction.

Grapevine: How many AA members are there in Colombia, and how many groups?

María Inés: We estimate that there are over 900 groups in Colombia and that we have between 15,000 and 18,000 alcoholics in recovery.

Grapevine: How does the Office carry the message to the alcoholic who's still suffering?

María Inés: The Office is the go-between because we work with the area committees, with the intergroup to whom we are constantly sending all the information that comes into the Office; we share with the delegates, especially during the Conference and through the entire year, through the reports we prepare. Also, we make sure that the people become more and more knowledgeable so that they can take the message to a greater segment of the population and to more areas.

Grapevine: Is there an effort being made to take the message to prisons, the countryside, or remote areas?

María Inés: Yes. The Office has just published the "Manual for

Institutions" and the "Manual for CCP" to be used by committees through our action plan. It's a plan of action created by the Board and which was approved by the 32nd Conference of General Services and which we are actively implementing. We've reached prisons despite the fact that many correctional facilities have closed their doors to our members because there were other people who, pretending to be AAs, entered the jails to give materials and weapons to the prisoners so they could escape. This situation has made things harder.

Grapevine: How does Colombian society perceive recovering alcoholics?

María Inés: I'd say we're well-accepted. Colombian society rejoices when people enter recovery and when they see that change in attitude toward life as we become useful people to our families and to society at large.

Grapevine: Is there a national awareness of what AA is, of what it does for the still suffering alcoholic?

María Inés: Of course there is. We've tried to do more public awareness campaigns. It's possible the Fellowship in Colombia is a little too anonymous and now we've been working with the Committee of Public Information, with the radio stations and television stations so that they run our ads and we can reach a greater number of people. At the entrance of the big cities we have billboards that give information about the Fellowship of Alcoholics Anonymous, with our telephone numbers so that those who are interested can call us. Some people have come into our rooms thanks to these efforts.

Grapevine: In your opinion, what are the main problems that AA faces in your country?

María Inés: The apathy of people toward giving service. People don't want to do any kind of service. We have very few leaders. The people who give service in the groups tend to be the same ones.

147

Grapevine: How's the situation of young people in AA? Are there many of them coming in right now?

María Inés: Young people of both sexes are more aware of AA and they are entering recovery more and more.

Grapevine: Ideally, what would you like to see happening for Colombian AA in the future?

María Inés: The Ministry of Health has published an estimate that there are six million active alcoholics in Colombia. If we could reach even a sixth of those people, that would be a great achievement. It means there's a great deal of work to do. We need to carry the message a little faster because the disease of alcoholism in Colombia is growing very fast, more quickly than the help that AA is giving. So we'd like to be ahead of it.

Grapevine: Why do you think alcoholism is spreading so fast?

María Inés: Because nowadays young people start drinking much earlier. In the past people started drinking when they were eighteen or twenty years old. Now there are those who at ten or twelve have already begun to drink alcoholically.

Grapevine: María Inés, could you talk about the road you've travelled in your recovery. How has alcohol affected your personal relations — with family, with friends, with your Fellowship?

María Inés: When I came into AA I hadn't lost my family, or my job, or many friends — I still had my circle of friends. What I had lost was faith in myself, inner peace, and the desire to live. I still had the material things, but my inner peace was completely gone, and that's what moved me to come into AA: eventually I came to a place where I didn't want to live or to drink. Then ensued total confusion, and I asked for help.

Since that time, I've remained in the group Los Doce Pasos,

which is near my house. From the first year it was not so hard for me because I accepted guidance. I let others sponsor me, I attended many meetings. And I saw that life at home became tranquil because my mother stopped worrying about my self-destruction and that moment when she'd no longer be there to save me from my chaos. My family was very happy with me; I started to have faith again; the will to live was restored. I experienced peace and serenity and I began to work my recovery program in earnest. And in AA I met my husband. I'm a fifty-four-year-old woman and three years ago I married an AA member who's been sober for twenty-eight years. This has been a beautiful part of my life.

Since I entered AA, my life has changed completely. I've felt my Higher Power, God as I conceive him, lead me every step of the way. And even though I've faced severe difficulties, too, with God's Grace I've been able to deal with them, always keeping in mind the principles of recovery of AA. That's why I think I've been able to do my job here in the General Service Office, because here you need someone with nerves of steel. Alcoholics love to criticize, to attack, and it wasn't easy for many to see a woman running this place for the first time. However, I've had the support of people, I've worked with honesty, and the Fellowship once again believes in the Office and wishes to help and support it.

Grapevine: How do Colombians see a woman in an important post, or has this no importance?

María Inés: Of course it does. The Office was run by men for thirty-seven years. So it was not easy to get them to accept me. Besides, there were several men who had applied for the job and only two women. It wasn't easy. But perhaps my experience, the knowledge I had acquired of the Office in the two years I worked as an Assistant of the Director, maybe all these things led the Board to give me this opportunity. But there were many men who didn't believe that this was a job for a woman; they said that the job required a man with a strong backbone! Nonetheless, I've been here two years, and I think God has helped me and guided me.

Grapevine: What are the most important changes you see in yourself as the years go by and you remain sober?

María Inés: Total acceptance of what I am going through. An enjoyment of life. Today I value much more what I am doing, my job, and the work that others do. It's also a beautiful thing to get to know — through the phone calls and letters we receive — about the need for a growing Office that reaches the still suffering alcoholic. This has been one of my greatest satisfactions: to serve others through the General Service Office, but always guided by God.

Grapevine: What message would you like to send our readers from Colombia?

María Inés: As a Colombian, but even more so as a member of the Fellowship, my message is one of unity, of humility. I'm becoming aware that the hardest thing for a recovering alcoholic is to work in unity, to work with love, without trying to be a big shot within the Fellowship. Also, the Office needs contributions so that we can reach more people. There are many people who need us, but the lack of funds limits what we can do. It's possible that not all of the groups nor the members are aware of the need to send contributions to the General Service Office so that we can work not just for Colombia but to sponsor other countries as well, and our message can be carried all over the world.

Grapevine: María Inés, thank you very much for your time. Is there anything else you'd like to say by way of conclusion?

María Inés: Yes, to the Grapevine readers I want to say that the Office of General Services in Colombia will always have its doors open to receive them and we welcome their visits and their help so we can continue to carry the message to more and more people.

(January 1999)

A Smiling Man, a Happy Man

Warsaw, Poland

Adam B. lives in Warsaw, Poland, and has been sober since January 1984. He was interviewed by telephone by a Grapevine staff member who began by asking him how he first came into AA.

Adam B.: My father and my wife brought me to a doctor because of problems with my drinking and my health. In those years, the level of knowledge of alcoholism among physicians and hospitals wasn't very high. I had a lot of luck to see a doctor who was very well informed about alcoholism, who knew about AA and knew how AA sees alcoholism. He told me briefly about AA.

Grapevine: Tell us a little bit about drinking in Poland.

Adam B.: Compared with the States, I believe, Poles drink much more, much bigger amounts of hard stuff. Vodka is the Polish national drink and we mostly drink vodka straight. It is the habit to drink vodka from youth onward.

Grapevine: How old were you when you started drinking?

Adam B.: I was a kid — sixteen years old. But until I was eighteen, I didn't drink too much. Before then, I was drinking only very occasionally. I came from so-called good family. There was no alcohol in my home. Father didn't drink too much and Mother hated drinking.

Grapevine: Do most people in Poland drink in bars?

Adam B.: During Communist time, restaurants and bars of not so good quality were usually full of people. Vodka was not expensive at that time. It was also very popular to drink vodka at home with friends

151

and family. Not as a "long drink," but straight up.

Grapevine: What has been the main impact on AA of the Solidarity movement and the free elections in 1989?

Adam B.: As I remember, the first AA group in Poland was start- ed in 1974. Poland was always quite different from Czechoslovakia, Soviet Union, or East Germany. The regime here was not so hard. I can't say that it was very easy to develop AA but we were not punished. There was no repression against AA. The secret police didn't arrest people.

A few months ago, I was in Slovakia and I was told that one Slovak lady in AA said, "The Poles were much more brave than we were." But it was not a great risk to join AA during the Communist regime. The political changes did not result in greater freedom for AA because we were already free to meet and to organize.

Grapevine: But hasn't democratization made it possible for more people to come into AA?

Adam B.: Yes. In March 1989, before the regime fell, we had about 300 AA groups in Poland. Today we have around 1,100 group names and addresses registered at the National Service Office. At the time AA started, it was completely impossible for example to establish a National Service Office because of laws regulating financing. Many people were afraid if we applied to the Communist government for incorporation, we'd be too much controlled.

Grapevine: By the state?

Adam B.: By authority. You come from society in which you learned free-market economy since you were a child. We did not have the experience of what it means to earn money, what it means to bud- get, what it means to organize. Because you know, in the Communist system, everything is granted from childhood. You don't need to think, you don't need to have political opinions. You are granted schools, you are granted jobs. But this system used to kill our initiative. This is the difference between trying to grow an AA organization in a country like the United States or Great Britain compared with Poland. And if you go today to Czechoslovakia, to Russia, you will find that the biggest problem is that people don't know how to get organized because they were always organized by somebody else. Poland is a little different because the church was very powerful and tended to balance the authority of the state, and even during Communist times there was a lot of private enterprise.

Grapevine: But you still had a certain lack of taking initiative, is that what you're saying?

Adam B.: Maybe not initiative, because we Poles love to have initiative and even hold completely different opinions about issues, but I should say lack of experience in managing, in financing, in marketing. We want to organize, we want entrepreneurship and initiative, we're not afraid to do it, even in Communist times, but we simply did not know how to do it. Poles have always had a history of making resistance. And in taking many things with some sense of humor, not so seriously.

Grapevine: When did you finally establish an independent legal corporation?

Adam B.: In January 1996. This is the National Service Office of Alcoholics Anonymous. But according to Polish law this is established as a foundation. In this legal form, we can follow all Traditions and all Concepts.

Grapevine: Did you have a problem with some of the Traditions in the early years?

Adam B.: I think that generally among Polish AA members there was a great support to follow the Traditions, not to break them. Of course I know of situations where sometimes they were broken. But this happens all over the world.

Grapevine: How did you educate yourself about the Traditions? Do you have Traditions meetings in Poland?

Adam B.: Very few, I'd have to say. But I can do what I've done by myself. First of all I've read the Traditions in the "Twelve and Twelve" and also pamphlets about the Traditions, and I speak a little English so I've had the opportunity to talk with Americans about the Traditions — in fact, about all organizational issues in AA.

Grapevine: How many of your groups support your National Service Office?

Adam B.: It's rather difficult to estimate because in Poland groups very often give money to their intergroups and then the intergroups send money to National Service Office.

Grapevine: Are intergroups a part of your service structure?

Adam B.: Yes. Right now we have over forty-five intergroups and each intergroup sends three delegates to the General Service Conference. However, we are going to change the structure and organize the structure with regions. Each region will send delegate members to General Service Conference. The decision about this will probably take place at the General Service Congress in August, and will become policy next year. So by August 1997, we'll have twelve regions each electing four members to the General Service Conference.

Grapevine: Have you had some problems brought up at the Congress that were difficult to solve?

Adam B.: Well, because of not having contact with GSO and lacking experience, we had to make many mistakes dealing with organization and financial problems. Let's say we were learning by mistakes, quite frankly. But always, always, our General Service

Conference and each two years our Congress, were very well represented by AA groups. It was always a good relation between the
Conference, the General Service Board, and the AA Fellowship as a
whole. Of course, there were many discussions, there were many differences, because sometimes people had differing ideas. There were
always resentments. But we never risked a situation where AA might
be divided. Alcoholics are sick people emotionally, so there were quarrels, there were very difficult discussions. But I can tell you, there was
never a risk that Polish AA might divide.

Grapevine: Do you have more meetings in the cities than in the
countryside?

Adam B.: Definitely. Our AA started in the big cities, but suddenly after a few years of being in AA, people started coming from
small cities, so it's now quite widely spread in Poland and you can now
find AA meetings in many small cities.

Grapevine: Are there more men than women in the Fellowship in
Poland?

Adam B.: Of course. I think that if we say seventy percent of AA
members are men, we may be right, but it's a very, very rough estima-
tion, not based on any kind of research.

Grapevine: You know in the United States, we've had a kind of
explosion of young people coming into AA. Do you see that also in
Poland?

Adam B.: Definitely. I remember when I came into AA it was
impossible to see any young men because at that time a man had to
suffer many, many years and go to a very low bottom before deciding
to go to AA. But in the meantime, knowledge about alcoholism and
the Fellowship of AA in Poland has grown so much that now there are
more and more young people at AA meetings — those who are not
more than twenty years old.

Another thing that helped spread the word about AA was the first TV program about AA — I mean interviews with AA people — which was on Communist TV around 1985. And there was an excellent article published that year called "Sin or Disease?" which could be compared to the Jack Alexander article in your country. It was written by Victor O., and it was based on his visit to the International Convention in Montreal. It was published in the Communist party magazine, which was the number one weekly magazine in Poland. So you can see that this regime was not so hard. This could never happen in neighboring countries.

Grapevine: After this article appeared, did a lot of people come into AA?

Adam B.: Yes. And it also made AA familiar to doctors, and to opinion makers, because it was published in a very serious weekly magazine. I'm glad to say that in many cities right now you can find information in newspapers about AA telephone numbers. For example, the largest daily newspaper in Warsaw publishes the addresses of two or three AA groups that are meeting that day. And if you came to Warsaw, you could open the phone book and find an AA telephone service.

Grapevine: What about sponsorship? Was the idea of sponsorship an important part of Alcoholics Anonymous to you when you came into the Fellowship in Poland?

Adam B.: Personally, I think sponsorship today should be at a higher level than it is. It's not so popular as it is in your country.

Grapevine: Why not?

Adam B.: I don't know. I myself decided to get a sponsor when I was eight years sober because I realized that on my own I'm too lazy, I'm making some mistakes, I'm not growing spiritually. So how can I criticize other people who don't have a sponsor?

Grapevine: Did you find someone who had more sobriety time than you did?

Adam B.: No, my life problem was that I came to AA after big mental disorders — being completely broken. I was pretty sure that I was zero in business, I knew I couldn't drink because it would kill me, but I thought I couldn't have anything in the business that I knew. I believed I would have to stay as a simple man, maybe as a worker, not as a businessman. But after half a year of so called sobriety — I was just staying dry, you know — I got a really well-paid job in a high position. It helped me to establish my financial issues, but I don't think it helped me in growing spiritually.

Grapevine: Why not?

Adam B.: As I see it today, it was too early. I wasn't emotionally prepared, not emotionally mature. Today I can say I'd rather have received this offer after two years in AA, not six months. Now, after eight years I realize that I've made so many mistakes. I was sometimes so far from living the AA way of life that when I was finally kicked in the butt I realized something was wrong. The best university for me — the best school, the best teaching — was in analyzing mistakes that I'd made and problems I created because of these mistakes. Not my successes, because during first eight years in AA I had some successes in business, but definitely they were taking me away from living AA way of life. This changed when I decided to get a sponsor and to work the Steps with him very well. And you know this man came to Alcoholics Anonymous I think two or three months after me, so it was for me some kind of being humble to ask him. This man, also named Adam — I always bless him. He helped me a lot, he was an excellent sponsor.

Grapevine: He's no longer your sponsor?

Adam B.: We don't meet. Right now I'm quite busy. We should meet from time to time. It's my mistake.

Grapevine: Do you have any sponsees?

Adam B.: No.

Grapevine: You're married?

Adam B.: I'm married to my wife Christina. Many, many years ago, I asked her to be my wife when I was drunk. It's the only good thing that I've done being drunk. She's a wonderful woman and passionate. During my alcoholism she was suffering with such a great passion and silence that I will always remember that. She's an excellent wife.

Grapevine: And how does she feel about AA? Does she feel good about it?

Adam B.: At the beginning she understood even better than I did how it could help. And she used to support me to go to AA meetings. In the first months it was very, very important you know.

Grapevine: How many AA meetings did you go to when you first started out?

Adam B.: As I remember, when I joined AA, there were three meetings in Warsaw for the whole week. Then we started group number four, so during my first year in AA there were meetings on Monday, Tuesday, Wednesday, and Thursday.

Grapevine: You have more to choose from now?

Adam B.: Today there are over 15 meetings every day in Warsaw which makes a total of about 105. Two of these meetings are in English.

Grapevine: Do you go to the English-speaking meetings sometimes?

Adam B.: I used to go quite frequently. It depends. Sometimes I go to Polish-speaking meetings, sometimes to English-speaking meetings. There's an English-speaking meeting on Mondays and I like it because for the first half hour we read the Big Book and discuss it.

Grapevine: Are most of your meetings an hour long?

Adam B.: Usually one and a half hours.

Grapevine: And do you have speakers?

Adam B.: In Warsaw there are two or three speakers meetings. There's a very big speaker meeting on Wednesday evening which always has about 200 people.

Grapevine: Do many meetings carry literature? I know you have the Big Book in Polish and the "Twelve and Twelve."

Adam B.: The "Twelve and Twelve" was translated into Polish in 1986 the first good translation. The Big Book came later. In the early days, literature was distributed illegally — it was printed illegally and distributed illegally because it was impossible to incorporate AA. So we were doing it unofficially, which meant we were breaking all financial laws. We didn't pay taxes for example. But nobody punished us.

Grapevine: Did the authorities know you were doing it?

Adam B.: Of course! I met some people from police headquarters and they knew very well about us. In a Communist regime, the Police had to know everything. And if they'd wanted us to stop doing it, we would have. But they simply didn't want to stop us.

Grapevine: We're coming to a close. Is there anything you'd like to say in conclusion?

Adam B.: I want to say that for me in the beginning here in

Warsaw it was a great story to meet Americans with many years of sobriety coming from the States. They helped us to understand the program, they shared their experience. During my first years in AA, I was sure that the AA way of life was something I couldn't understand. Someone would say, "I'm happy to be alcoholic," and I wanted to kill him. How can an alcoholic be happy? How can an alcoholic be smiling? But from friends from the States coming here and writing here, I came to understand the joy of life, that an alcoholic can be a smiling, happy man.

I also want to mention a man I'll always remember, Jack L. from New Jersey. Jack came to Polish AA meetings, and we became friends. He was probably one of my best friends, a man with whom I was sharing so much. He was like my sponsor. He used to come to Poland two times a year to do business here, and we'd spend hours and hours talking about life. He passed away in 1990. When I got the message of his death, I started to cry. He was such an important man in my life. I just want to honor him.

(October 1996)

———◎———

LIFE IS HARD ENOUGH ALREADY

Nairobi, Kenya

Abongo O. got sober in January 1989 in Washington, D.C., and in April 1995 he returned to his native Kenya to make his home in Nairobi. He was interviewed by telephone by a Grapevine staff member.

Grapevine: Tell us about the differences between AA in Kenya and AA as you experienced it in the States.

Abongo O.: In D.C., each group had a chairman, secretary, treasurer, and maybe a coffee maker, a GSR, and intergroup and Grapevine representatives. Over here, the secretary and treasurer and coffee maker are sort of voluntary — at the end of the meeting we ask for volunteers. So it's different that way; the organization is not as elaborate. After all, Alcoholics Anonymous only began in Kenya twenty-five years ago. But I'd say our meetings are first-class. We have several groups and it's possible to have a meeting daily.

Grapevine: How many meetings do you have in Nairobi?

Abongo O.: We have about fifteen groups.

Grapevine: Are there AA meetings out in the country?

Abongo O.: There are a few meetings upcountry. I've had the opportunity to go to where I come from, and I found a member of Alcoholics Anonymous in the village. That was really a discovery. So you can tell everybody that AA is all the way to the villages.

Grapevine: How did the person in your village find AA?

Abongo O.: Where I came from is called Siaya district, and the main town is called Siaya Town, and in that town there's a meeting on Sunday. I think it was started by some members of the church.

Grapevine: What sort of literature do you have available in meetings? Do you have the Big Book in the Kenyan tongue?

Abongo O.: Yes, we have the Big Book in Kiswahili, and also the "Twelve and Twelve," which was translated and printed here. We need support as far as literature is concerned. We need more literature in Kiswahili and English too. Right now the Big Book in Kiswahili is fourteen dollars. It's much more expensive than the traditional English version. If we had it printed out here, it would be much cheaper. But we'd need more of an organizational structure and the approval of GSO.

Grapevine: Are there treatment centers in Kenya? Do doctors refer alcoholics to AA or treatment centers?

Abongo O.: Yes, the doctors are aware of the existence of Alcoholics Anonymous and also are knowledgeable about alcoholism. And there are facilities. I definitely know of one where they treat alcoholics, and alcoholics are referred to them by a psychiatrist. I also know of a doctor who's involved in helping alcoholics get admission into the hospital. Some alcoholics are taken to the mental institution.

Grapevine: How did the doctors and hospitals get informed about AA? Do you have any public information activity going on?

Abongo O.: We've been trying to get an intergroup organized here, we've had a problem with participation. The groups are okay but a lot of groups are self-sufficient and not really into service beyond the group level. Sometimes there's participation and things are happening, and then it tapers off and nothing goes on and people don't turn up. But there is a meeting list for Kenya, there's a help desk or a telephone number, so somebody can call if they have a problem. But participation is not really running as it should.

Grapevine: In what way should it function better?

Abongo O.: The spirit of service is not emphasized. There's one man who's been instrumental in getting an intergroup started here but when he's not around, then nothing can get done. There's no real organized way of getting groups informed at that level. And apart from the intergroup, there's no service structure here. But about four of us have continued to meet, and we've scheduled a workshop next month. The theme is "The Spirit of Sacrifice" and we're going to discuss sponsorship, group service, general service, and Step work.

Grapevine: If we came to Nairobi and wanted to go to AA meeting, could we look in the phone book and find Alcoholics Anonymous?

Abongo O.: AA meetings are listed in the newspaper. One of our dailies, the *Daily Nation*, has a section called "information service" and the meeting for that day is included in that.

Grapevine: Tell us about the makeup of the meetings.

Abongo O.: We have people who are working here from all over the world. And so we have Americans, Britons, Asians and of course indigenous Kenyans. And because some people speak Kiswahili, are more fluent in Kiswahili, we have both Kiswahili meetings and English meetings. I'm afraid also that we have some cliques where the members stick together — especially those that are economically better off.

Grapevine: How does this affect AA in Kenya?

Abongo O.: I think that it does not auger well. Because there are resentments that occur, and so I'd say the unity of AA here needs to be better.

Grapevine: What would you like to see happen?

Abongo O.: The main thing we're trying to do is somehow spread the message that regardless of our status or background, there's a solution in Alcoholics Anonymous. It's not only for those who are economically better off. Whenever a drunk needs help we want the hand of AA to be there. Again, it's an issue of literature here. For example, we need some kind of guidelines on what AA stands for, what it is, and how it works, for some of these places where they are not as well off. So all the groups would know that even though they are self-supporting through their own contributions, they aren't completely on their own. So that all will feel that AA here is connected with AA worldwide. Because somewhat I find that AA in Kenya is isolated. I'd like to see AA in Kenya just as vibrant and just as well as AA anywhere, with a central office, a general service assembly or an area assembly, and maybe delegates. It's just a matter of one day at a time, keeping the principles in mind, the message in mind.

Grapevine: What is the attitude about alcohol and drinking in Kenya? What is it like in the villages?

Abongo O.: The attitude toward drunkenness is one of contempt and ridicule. Anybody who drinks the way we alcoholics drink is not considered any good for the society or for the village community, where life is hard enough already.

Grapevine: It's not part of tribal celebrations or holidays?

Abongo O.: You have to be licensed to offer alcohol publicly. If there is a funeral or something like that, okay. It depends on the kind of alcohol you're drinking because there is illegal alcohol brew.

Grapevine: What is it?

Abongo O.: There's *chang'aa*, there's *bus'aa*, and there's some others. These are made from grain, both fermented and distilled. *Chang'aa* is distilled — it's strong like whiskey.

Grapevine: So is this imbibed in the villages and small towns?

Abongo O.: It's more traditional in the villages. They've been making it for ages. It was made illegal by the authorities during the colonial era, but people continued to use it, of course, because bottled beer and imported whiskey are expensive.

Grapevine: Do more men than women show up at the meetings?

Abongo O.: A lot more male alcoholics turn up than female.

Grapevine: Why do you think that is?

Abongo O.: I'd think that it's the stigma associated with the woman drinking and maybe also the social structure — that women are supposed to be at home. It may be even an issue of not knowing where meetings are.

Grapevine: Do you think that there are as many female alcoholics as male ones?

Abongo O.: I know in a bar you'll find women drinking. Wherever drinks are being served you'll find a whole bunch of women, too. So, I'd say yes, there's just as many. But maybe there are not as many who can find the courage to come along, to get out of the closet, to reveal themselves, to come to the meetings.

Grapevine: What are the main problems that AA in Kenya faces now?

Abongo O.: It's just the lack of information. It's just going to take time to get the message across.

Grapevine: Abongo, we want to thank you for talking with us today.

Abongo O.: I'd just like to say that Alcoholics Anonymous is the best thing that can ever happen to anybody. I've been a member of Alcoholics Anonymous for over seven years and things are still happening to me. It makes me more and more aware that this is the life for me. AA is my life today. Everything is centered around Alcoholics Anonymous and not the other way around. And if there is anything I can do to pass the message I will, because everything I have I owe to Alcoholics Anonymous.

(October 1996)